Praise for Felicity Hayes-McCoy

'I felt a sense of wellbeing. I had walked with her
around the peninsula and experienced her wonder
and delight. The book glowed with an appreciation
of her lifestyle in Dingle.'
Alice Taylor

'Powerful ... reflecting on life with an inquiring
intelligence and emotional honesty.'
The Sunday Times

'There is something entirely Irish about her writing
... the soft wild country of the Dingle Peninsula
comes alive. Completely enchanting.'
Joanna Lumley

'Thought-provoking ... immensely entertaining.'
Irish Examiner

'Outstanding.'
Sunday Independent

Herding sheep on a road above Ballyferriter.

DINGLE AND ITS HINTERLAND
People, Places and Heritage

Felicity Hayes-McCoy, originally from Dublin, also writes novels, and for radio, television, music theatre and digital media. Her father was the historian G. A. Hayes-McCoy. With her husband, the English opera director **Wilf Judd**, she divides her life and work between a flat in inner city London and a stone house at the western end of the Dingle Peninsula.

 @felicity hayes-mccoy

 @fhayesmccoy

 felicityhayesmccoy.co.uk

To our friends and neighbours in Dingle and 'back west'
Ar scáth a chéile a mhaireann na daoine.

Mount Brandon from Béal Bán.

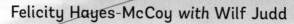

Felicity Hayes-McCoy with Wilf Judd

DINGLE AND ITS HINTERLAND

People, Places and Heritage

The Collins Press

First published in 2017 by
The Collins Press
West Link Park
Doughcloyne
Wilton
Cork
T12 N5EF
Ireland

A CIP record for this book is available from the British Library.

Paperback ISBN: 978-1-84889-308-5
PDF eBook ISBN: 978-1-84889-629-1
EPUB eBook ISBN: 978-1-84889-630-7
Kindle ISBN: 978-1-84889-631-4

Design and typesetting by Studio 10
Typeset in Chaparral pro
Printed in Poland by Białostockie Zakłady Graficzne SA

Photograph on pp ii–iii: Generations of manual labour have cleared
land for agricultural use and provided stone for building.

CONTENTS

Wild honeysuckle.

Introduction

The entrance to Dingle Harbour.

THIS BOOK AIMS to draw the reader into a deeper understanding and appreciation of the history and heritage of the
western end of the Dingle Peninsula by offering not just facts
and illustrations but personal views and experiences shared
by people who live here. The core of each chapter is transcribed from
a conversation between the authors and individuals who range from
farmers and fishermen, musicians and teachers to a seafarer and
boatbuilder, a chef, a broadcaster, a postmaster, a traditional *sean-
nós* singer and a museum curator. We are deeply grateful to everyone
who took time to sit at our kitchen table, or welcomed us into their
own homes and workplaces, to make these recordings. We also owe
a huge debt of gratitude to the many other individuals who offered
stories, advice on the pronunciation guide, memories, facts and
photographs, stopped us on high cliffs, sandy beaches and street
corners, and sent texts and emails with additional remarks,
information and insights.

In writing a guide to an area with a history that stretches back
into prehistory, and an oral culture that offers myriad variations of
stories, tunes, folklore and place names, we were inevitably faced

with decisions as to what to include and what to leave out. Since our purpose is to encourage a deeper, more nuanced understanding of the area, we have made those decisions on the basis of offering readers a series of starting points for further conversations and for much enjoyable exploration of their own. Because, as everyone who has ever come to the western end of the Dingle Peninsula has discovered, one book or conversation or visit is never enough.

Choices also had to be made when deciding how best to convey the meaning and pronunciation of words and phrases in the Irish language. Generally, the English-language version of an Irish place name is either an anglicisation of its original Irish-language name or a direct or partial translation of it. ('An Muiríoch' becomes 'Murreagh', for example, and 'Baile Dháith', 'Ballydavid'). As a rule of thumb, as our route takes us west along the Slea Head Drive, we have given the Irish-language name first when a place is first mentioned in the text, followed by its Anglicisation or translation in brackets. Overall, however, we opted for clarity over consistency and broke our rule where more explanation seemed necessary or interesting or where the English-language version is generally used locally. A guide to approximate pronunciations of Irish-language words is included at the back of the book.

The Irish and English forms of given names and surnames are often interchangeable, both in Dingle, where Irish is frequently spoken, and in the rural area beyond the town, known simply as 'back west', where it's the first language of everyday life. This can occur regardless of which language is being spoken, so Máire Nic Gearailt can become Mary Fitzgerald – or Séamas Sullivan, Jim Ó Súilleabháin – within the same sentence. We have given the forms of individuals' names as they were given to us, and clarified where it seemed necessary. It is worth noting here that, though standardised spelling exists in Irish, vernacular spelling is often still used, in particular where names are concerned.

But none of this matters when you let down your car window and ask for directions, or sit over a pint or a coffee chatting to local people. At the western end of the Dingle Peninsula the visitor's experience is all the richer for the fact that the locality's wealth of information, wit, wisdom and humour is expressed in not one but two languages.

Dingle Town

The harbour

Main Street

Dingle was once an important port on one of Europe's medieval trading routes.

THE STREETS OF DINGLE TOWN speak of how life is lived here; their narrow pavements require you to take your time and meet people's eyes. You smile and step aside on the pavements and nod to the drivers on the road who pause and signal to let you cross. If you're driving a car yourself you'll notice that people approaching each other raise one finger from the steering wheel; it's a salute that goes back to the time when every stranger and friend was greeted here with the same formal courtesy and every encounter was cause to stop for a chat.

A traditional readiness to engage with passers-by is part of the charm of the area. In the town, where the streets are often crowded in summer, you soon learn to take things a bit slower and to appreciate the rhythms of a different kind of life. The presence of the cattle mart on the Spa Road or the fact that the town has an active and vocal Fishermen's Association can easily go unnoticed by a casual observer, yet they testify to an age-old involvement in farming and fishery that continues to the present day: and the combination of the locals' culture of conversation with their knowledge of the land and the ocean is a gift to the curious visitor.

The Dingle Peninsula stretches westwards about 50km into the Atlantic Ocean, with the Blasket Islands as an offshore extension of the mainland ridge. Its mountainous spine extends from Sliabh Mis (Slieve Mish) in the east to the transverse bulk of Cnoc Breannáin (Mount Brandon), the gateway to Dingle town, in the west. Beyond the town, and bisected by a high pass, are Sliabh an Iolair (Mount Eagle) and Cruach Mhárthain (Croagh Marhin), its most westerly mountains. The coastline is irregular and, along its length, the

Dingle Pier has long served as a haven for Irish and foreign fishing boats in stormy weather.

Dingle town, looking west.

The statue of Fungie, Dingle's Dolphin.

peninsula varies between 6 and 20km in width from north to south, with no point more than 8km from the ocean.

Dingle town has a population of around 2,000, significantly increased in summer by the presence of visitors, and by part-time workers in the hospitality industry. At the head of the pier, close to the Tourist Information Office, is a bronze statue of Fungie the dolphin, arguably the town's most famous character. His story exemplifies both the happenstance that characterises so much of Dingle life and the extent to which humans and the natural world exist here in harmony.

In the early 1980s fishermen at the harbour mouth began to notice a young bottle-nosed dolphin following their boats. Schools of dolphin and other marine life are frequently sighted in the area but this individual was no passer-by. Instead he showed an increasing

GREEN STREET, DINGLE

A 1950s postcard of Dingle's Green Street, looking towards the nineteenth-century Roman Catholic church of St Mary. COURTESY CATHY CORDUFF

interest in the boats and in sub-aqua divers. And eventually he became the focus of a major tourist attraction. As commercial fishing declined, trips to see Fungie began booming. And, in time, he began to give thrilling displays of leaping and dancing with a sense of awareness and comic timing that make it hard to believe that the choreography is his own: so much so, that local people are well used to visitors asking when the dolphin is fed or where the boatmen keep him. But Fungie is a wild dolphin. No one trained him. He hunts for his food and his interaction with humans is his own choice. That fact is a good starting point for remembering that the western end of the Dingle Peninsula is not a theme park but a living landscape. It's a place with a rich and unique cultural inheritance that can best be explored not just through the usual interfaces provided for tourists but through relaxed conversation with the people who live and work here.

CONVERSATION:
Cormac O'Sullivan

For Cormac O'Sullivan, the manager of Benners Hotel in Main Street, Dingle town's historic importance as a port is what gives it its unique character.

❧ Look at its physical position, on a trading route that's brought people here for over a thousand years. Ships came in bringing leather and wine and goods from all over Europe, and even beyond. They brought new ideas, they came here and they talked to people. Sure, three hundred years ago there were Spanish merchants that set up house here, so the town's exposure to new cuisines and cultures goes way back in time. Because of its geographical position and the mountain passes you have to cross to get to it, you might say it was isolated. But the sea always linked it to the rest of the world. ❧

The hotel Cormac manages is the oldest in Dingle town. Sometime in the early 1700s the Benner family arrived in Ireland from the Palatinate region of south-western Germany, and came to Kerry in the 1740s. Having worked as brewers and distillers, one branch of the family became innkeepers and are recorded as successful hoteliers in Tralee in the 1780s. In 1896 Robert Benner and his wife, Georgina Revington, daughter of a prominent Kerry retailer, established Benners Hotel in Dingle. Robert died relatively young but the Benner empire continued to expand and Georgina continued to run the Dingle hotel; the 1911 census shows her there as a widow with six live-in servants including a car-man and a nurse. Today the hotel is still housed in the building that Georgina and her husband came to as newly-weds. With a significant extension to the rear, its elegant door and reception rooms still face onto Main Street and, though now under the ownership of a US group, it retains the historic Benner name.

DINGLE TOWN

7

Like Robert and Georgina, Cormac is an incomer to the Dingle area.

❝ I was born in Limerick but I spent every summer here. My father attended an Irish-language course west of Dingle town in the 1950s, my parents honeymooned there, and the family went from staying in tents, to caravans, to a mobile home and, eventually, to building our own house. I started in the hotel business washing pots in a hotel back west and, after going off to work elsewhere in Ireland, I came back.

That was my experience but it's often the same for local people. Because we're surrounded by the ocean, people born and bred here have always travelled. There was a time when this was one of the most isolated regions of Ireland in one sense, because it's at the very end of a peninsula at the westernmost edge of mainland Europe. And that's why so much of its ancient native culture has been preserved. But it wouldn't have survived if the people who lived here hadn't survived themselves. There's always been huge emigration, with people travelling to find work. And I suppose kids will always want to go off and see the world. But they come back, and I think that movement is what brings life to the place. Like, if you think of the music round here and you think of an accordion – you draw it out and you push it back and you bring air into it, and it's the movement in and out that makes the music.

The people are shaped by the landscape, the landscape is shaped by the people and there's an instinct there to help and support each other. It's a tourist town with a strong local infrastructure supporting it. If you're stuck for something you need and you go up to Foxy John's at eleven at night they'll dodge

The window of Foxy John's famous pub and hardware store.

over from the bar counter to the hardware counter and get it for you. There's a kind of a rhythm you have to get used to, though. Life here happens when it happens and it takes the time it takes. Trying to make it happen doesn't make it happen any quicker.

When The Irish Food Awards, Blas na hÉireann, were set up in 2006 Dingle became Ireland's "Foodie Town". We won the title in the inaugural year and since then we've been host to the annual awards ceremony. There are Gold, Silver and Bronze Awards in over a hundred food and drink categories, and key awards such as Supreme Champion and Best Artisan Producer and the whole thing takes place over a long  weekend in October. As far as I'm concerned, the relationship between the town and Food Awards is a match made in heaven.

There's so much enterprise in the area now, between individuals and larger businesses, and lots of it food and drink related. And, because Dingle people are well-travelled, we're used to new ideas coming in – experimentation is part of what life's about. That's manifested in the restaurants, the farmer's market, the Dingle Cookery School – people here have taken what's around them and taken it to the next level. Food is field to fork, sea to plate. We have locally fished seafood, and meat sold by butchers who are farmers. There's salt-fed lamb grazed out on the Blasket Islands and Dingle Dexter cattle thriving up on the mountains. People know the dates when farmers would be moving livestock on the roads, buying and selling at the mart

Local craft butcher and farmer Jerry Kennedy is a Blas na hÉireann Gold Award winner.

here in town. Agriculture is all around us. Even in the supermarkets you have local produce and great support for local producers. And the purpose of the Food Festival is to showcase what's local to the place, and to bring producers from other parts of the country together, to share ideas and cross-fertilise knowledge.

The judging and prize-giving for the Irish Food Awards take place during the town's own annual Food

Dingle Food Festival, which promotes local produce, fills every street in town.

Festival, which is run by volunteers. So food and drink really are the focus of the weekend. We have street stalls all over town, and a Taste Trail for which you buy tickets that let you sample food and drink in over sixty outlets that vary from pubs and galleries to shops and restaurants. And there's music events, cookery workshops and demonstrations, and street entertainment. Much of that would be free and all the profits from paid events are donated to charity.

And that's great because the tourist industry is the town's largest employer. But it also gives visitors a chance to enjoy more than one season here. Our weather is changeable at the best of times – they say you can get four seasons in a single day – but it's a fact that some of the best weather can happen in autumn. So visitors come for the Food Festival, or later in the month for Halloween, which originated as a Celtic seasonal festival, and they enjoy the area when things might be more quiet. And you always get people round for New Year's and home for Christmas.

Christmas lights on Main Street.

Dingle Oceanworld Aquarium.

The marina on an autumn evening.

You get fewer people coming on day trips in spring and autumn. If I'm asked, what I always say is that you can't get the best out of Dingle in a day anyway. You need to take your time, stay longer and make the place your own. Ask your concierge about where to go and what to do. There's indoor things, like the Aquarium and the Play at Height climbing wall, if it's raining or if you've kids with you.

And go into the west. The time to send people back to Slea Head is in the afternoon, when it's quieter, or in the evening, when they'll get the sunset. One thing we have here is light – we have light till after ten o'clock at night in summer and, before the clocks go back, in autumn you can still have it at seven. There's stress and hard work involved in my work but, working here, I can drive home round Slea Head and by the time I'm home I'm completely relaxed. The light reflecting off the ocean and the colours in the sky make the stress just drain out of you – and you can't buy that. 🎵

Although the Irish language is spoken far more widely west of Dingle, where it's the first language of the people, you will see it written in signs in many of the shops and pubs in the town, and in some businesses you'll see a sign near the till that reads '*Tá cúpla focal agam*', which translates as 'I have a few words', indicating that whoever is serving speaks some Irish and will be delighted if customers use the language. In Irish '*Go raibh maith agat*' means 'thank you' and '*Slán*' means 'goodbye'. '*Dia dhuit*', which literally translates as 'God be with you', means 'Hello'.

'*Cúpla focal*' sign in a local shop.

The Courthouse pub, next to Dingle's Court House, on The Mall.

Seasonal festive celebrations are a tradition in Ireland, where rural communities are still linked to the rhythms of lives lived close to the earth and the ocean. In Dingle town they form part of a cultural fabric in which ancient ritual, conscious revival and comparatively recent innovation are interwoven.

The modern Food Festival takes place at a time of the year when harvest festivals were traditionally held across Europe, celebrating the gathering-in of produce to last rural communities through the winter. The music events that accompany it are part of a strong local tradition in which the oral inheritance of the area is passed on in music, song and storytelling; and any night of the week throughout the year you can find both organised and impromptu music sessions in many of the town's pubs. Music is also central to Dingle's St Patrick's Day celebrations, on 17 March, when fife-and-drum bands and traditional instrumentalists parade through the streets in honour of Ireland's patron saint. The town's May Festival, *Féile na Bealtaine,* celebrates the coming of summer with storytelling, song, dance, visual arts, literature and music, both traditional Irish and cosmopolitan.

In 2002 the first Other Voices event was recorded in St James' Church in Dingle's Main Street, spawning an international music series that marked its tenth anniversary with two shows at New York's Le Poisson Rouge. It returns to its Dingle roots each December, to record a television spectacular which mixes contemporary and traditional music and, over the years, has featured performances from artists as diverse as Amy Winehouse, Sinéad O'Connor, Snow Patrol, Rufus and Martha Wainwright and Jarvis Cocker.

Many of Dingle's longer-established events are echoes of seasonal gatherings that were part of the pre-Christian Celtic calendar. The town's annual horse races and the rowing regatta in the harbour take place in August, when festivals were traditionally held to honour the god Lugh; the three-day races are Ireland's largest horse and pony race meeting, and both it and the regatta are organised and run by local volunteers.

Dingle's largest and most famous seasonal festival has origins rooted in pre-Christian midwinter ritual across Europe and Scandinavia. *Lá an Dreóilín* was once a major feast throughout the country. Celebrated on 26 December, its name translates as The Wren's Day, linking it to the Christian legend of the wren that betrayed the martyr St Stephen, whose feast falls on the same date.

The Wren's Day in Dingle town combines modern charity collections with ancient ritual.

Throughout the day, groups of musicians and revellers parade the streets. Although identified with different parts of the town by the colours they wear, their costumes are disguises. They range from beautifully made straw masks and skirts to blackened faces and tattered clothing and, in many cases, men dress as women and vice versa, underlining the idea of a festival of Misrule. The groups are known collectively as 'Wrans' (from the local pronunciation of 'wren') and some carry a crudely made effigy of a horse; when they meet they stage mock stand-offs, encouraged by the onlookers. The festival was variously condemned and partially stamped out both by the Church and state authorities over the centuries. In its present form it has probably been influenced by medieval mummers' plays subsequently introduced to Ireland by English soldiers and settlers, whose own Christmas folk traditions were equally resonant of pre-Christian ritual. The Wren's Day in Dingle is very much a festival for the townspeople and money collected by the marchers is given to charity: photos and artefacts relating to it can be seen in many of the town's pubs and premises. Other, far smaller, Wrans walk and drive the roads and play music in pubs and houses farther west; often they're made up of groups of children who use the money they collect for the more traditional purpose of buying sweets and provisions for a party.

Dingle Library, on Green Street, had a complex genesis. In 1909 the MP for West Kerry successfully applied to The Carnegie Trust for a grant to establish a public library but it was not built until 1918

Entrance to Dingle Library and Thomas Ashe exhibit.

as no suitable site could be found in the town. Its opening was then delayed until a dispute over the lease of the site with the landlord, Lord Ventry, was resolved in 1928. It was not until 1934 that the building opened, incorporating into its collection about 100 volumes that had formed a lending library at The Dingle Temperance Hall. For a number of years the Carnegie building was also used as a community and social centre, and for dances and theatrical performances. It was renovated in the mid-1980s and now provides an adult and children's lending library, reference and study areas, exhibition facilities, public internet access, a range of audio-visual and computer equipment, and a fine collection of material, in both Irish and English, specifically related to the Dingle Peninsula. A small exhibition centred on Thomas Ashe, a local man who was one of the heroes of Ireland's 1916 Rising, was remounted to celebrate the centenary year.

Monsignor Pádraig Ó Fiannachta, an academic, poet and priest who was born in the locality and died here in 2016, was a professor of Early Irish and a Welsh Language lecturer in St Patrick's College Maynooth from the 1960s: he became Professor of Modern Irish there in 1982 and was the translator and editor of the only modern Bible in the Irish language, completed in the twentieth century, *An Bíobla Naofa* (An Sagart, 1981). In 1993 he presented Dingle Library with a large personal book collection of over 4,600 items. An extension was added to the rear of the building to house it. Thereafter, the Monsignor continued to add to the collection, which now has over 6,000 items. It includes facsimile editions of rare Irish manuscripts and annals, sets of learned journals, Irish dictionaries from the nineteenth and twentieth centuries and Greek readers that once belonged to Éamon de Valera. A wide and varied selection of subjects is covered including Irish literature, the Irish language, local history, archaeology, religion, hagiography, folklore, art, poetry and history. The books are in English, Irish, Latin, Welsh, Breton, Russian, German, French, Greek, Spanish, Korean and Japanese.

Books are sold in various gift shops and supermarkets in the town and Dingle has two thriving independent bookshops. One, in Green Street, keeps an extensive range of stock, for the general reader. The other, in Dykegate Lane, off Main Street, carries an

Looking north from Dykegate Lane towards Main Street.

equally broad range of books, and specialises in Irish-interest and Irish-language material. The McKenna family opened a café in Dykegate Lane in 1939 and for many years it was a popular eating place for farmers coming to town to sell cattle. In 1979 it became An Café Liteartha, 'The Literary Café', where politics and local affairs were discussed at the rear and books sold at the front. Its layout and appearance have hardly changed since then, and Seoirse Ó Luasa who owns and runs it is a fount of knowledge on Irish books and publishing.

Farther along Dykegate Lane is the 150-seat, family-run Phoenix Cinema which is one of the oldest independent cinemas in Ireland. Built with a sprung floor, the cinema doubled as the town's dance hall until the 1970s. Now it shows recently released films throughout the year, with Art Film Nights on Tuesdays, when tea and biscuits are served to the audience. The Dingle International Film Festival, which was founded in 2007, takes place annually in March: it promotes and platforms Irish film, filmmakers and animation, and plays host to major industry players from Ireland and abroad. The

Dykegate Lane, looking south towards the Phoenix Cinema.

festival's Gregory Peck Award for Excellence in the Art of Film is named for the Hollywood actor who, through his Irish-born paternal grandmother Catherine, was related to Thomas Ashe.

There is no native Irish tradition of theatre; it arrived from England, initially took hold in the cities in the eighteenth century, and has flourished in Ireland ever since. Dingle town has two theatres, one, at Cooleen, near the seafront, and the other further up the town, at the top of John Street. At Cooleen, the Beehive Theatre gives well-attended amateur performances in English. An Lab, in John Street, is housed in a space that was once the science lab of the former Christian Brothers' secondary school, a nineteenth-century building which closed as a school in 2007. It stages amateur and professional productions, mainly in the Irish language, presents art exhibitions, and holds concerts at lunchtimes and in the evenings; the mixed media flavour of its output reflects a fusion of local and imported performance tradition.

The extraordinary beauty of the area and the quality of the light reflected from the ocean have brought many professional and amateur artists to Dingle, and the town has several small galleries as well as shops selling works by local craftspeople and artists. Since 1998 The Díseart Institute of Education and Celtic Culture has occupied the nineteenth-century neo-Gothic building beside the Catholic church on Green Street, formerly home to an enclosed community of Presentation nuns. The convent chapel is lit by twelve windows commissioned by the sisters and designed and installed in the 1920s by the Dublin-born stained-glass artist and book illustrator Harry Clarke, a leading figure in the Irish Arts and Crafts Movement. Both the convent and church were designed by the Irish architect J. J. McCarthy; construction began on the church in 1868 and – as happened less radically to other churches across the country – its interior and exterior appearance was substantially altered in the 1960s in response to guidelines for reordering issued by the Second Vatican Council.

Many buildings in the town have stories attached to them. At the junction of Goat Street and Green Street, for example, is The Rice House, which in the eighteenth century belonged to James Louis Rice, a prosperous local wine merchant. Rice, who was educated in Belgium, joined the Austrian army and became an intimate friend of the Hapsburg emperor Joseph II, who made him a Count of the Holy Roman Empire. According to local tradition, during the French Revolution, when the emperor's sister Marie Antoinette was imprisoned with her family in Paris, Rice contrived to bribe her gaolers and arranged relays of horses to take her to the French coast, where one of his family's merchant ships was waiting to smuggle her to Dingle. Legend has it that rooms had been prepared for the queen at The Rice House but that, at the last moment, she refused to abandon her family, remaining with them in their prison in the Temple in Paris and dying with her husband on the guillotine.

The story of Dingle town itself is one of enterprise, struggle and adjustment; periods of peace and prosperity have alternated with times of unrest and extreme poverty, and the townspeople have a resilience born of that knowledge. They also have a deep respect for their own history, exemplified by the carefully maintained site of a mass graveyard on the hillside above the building that was once the town's workhouse. The site, which is reached via Chapel Lane, off Goat Street, and has car parking a short walk from the graveyard, is a place that Cormac O'Sullivan suggests to visitors seeking an insight into Dingle and its people. During the Great Famine of the 1840s the bodies of an estimated 8,000 men, women and children were buried here, in what is now a small green field bounded by low stone walls and flanked by a covered area with a view of the ocean and benches for prayer and contemplation. As well as the Famine victims, it was a burial ground for unknown drowned sailors and, in living memory, for stillborn babies. In 2016, interviewed by a local journalist, the volunteers who care for the site explained that they do so 'to honour the people buried here'. One man who knows that

members of his own family rest there in unmarked graves says that whenever he comes to cut grass and clear weeds at the graveyard he stays to speak to them. 'I talk to them. I do. Because their spirit is here.'

Dingle's Famine graveyard.

DINGLE TOWN

Dingle town was developed as a port after the twelfth-century Norman invasion of Ireland but it was certainly a centre of population from earlier times. Its name is a corruption of the Irish *Daingean Uí Chúis*, The Fortress of O'Cuis. The town is referred to in a thirteenth-century document as 'Dengynhuyss' and Ó Cúis is not a native surname, so 'Uí Chúis' may be an early corruption of the Flemish name Hussey, which came to the area with the Normans.

The Earls of Desmond, the Norman Fitzgerald family who ruled the area, became highly assimilated to the Irish native culture and, over time, developed close trading associations with Spain. By the sixteenth century, Dingle was one of Ireland's significant trading ports, exporting fish, hides and other goods to the continent of Europe and importing wines – a pier near the site of the modern marina was known as the Spanish Pier. The town also became a major embarkation port for pilgrims to the shrine of St James at Santiago de Compostela and the dedication of the parish church to St James is believed to date to that period. The current church on the site in Main Street is a nineteenth-century building.

Under the Tudors, Dingle and the western end of the peninsula became a centre of rebellion when Spanish and Papal Italian troops combined with the army of the Earls of Desmond in failed attempts to reject English, and assert Fitzgerald, rule in Munster.

The Marina Inn faces Dingle Pier.

Following the defeat of the Desmond Rebellion, the town was incorporated as a borough and enclosed with a wall pierced by several gates. (The name Dykegate Lane refers to this period: Dykegate, locally pronounced 'Dagget', is a corruption of the Irish '*dá geata*' – 'two gates'.) The area of jurisdiction of the borough's corporation was all land and sea within two Irish miles of the parish church, and its admiralty jurisdiction extended westwards to Ventry, Smerwick and Ferriter's Creek.

Having weathered periods of warfare and political unrest under the Stuarts and the Commonwealth, Dingle developed a flourishing linen industry in the eighteenth century. By the nineteenth century this had declined and the effects of the potato famine at a time of high unemployment were devastating.

After the setting up of the Irish state, widespread emigration and rural poverty continued in the area until well into the twentieth century when David Lean's 1970 film *Ryan's Daughter* sparked the beginning of a thriving tourist industry that, along with increased investment in local business and light industry, has contributed to the growth and redevelopment of the town.

ABOVE: Herring gull, Dingle Pier.

LEFT: Dingle Town Take-away.

2 Milltown and Burnham

Blight-resistant potato varieties are now a popular domestic crop on the peninsula.

Wild honeysuckle at the old estate at Burnham.

Summer meadow near Milltown.

THE ROUNDABOUT AT MILLTOWN
BRIDGE marks the entrance to a
discrete rural area, distinct from
Dingle town, that offers the
visitor some of the most spectacular
scenery on the peninsula as well as some
of the deepest insights into Ireland's
native cultural inheritance. Stretching
from Milltown to the extreme western
end of the land mass and north to
Brandon Creek, this is the area that is
known as 'back west'. Here Irish has been
the language of everyday life for millennia

Road sign at Milltown Bridge.

and continues to preserve and transmit a rich heritage of local
tradition, folklore, mythology, history, song and place lore. Both the
language itself and the culture it preserves survived and now
continue to flourish here despite the area's history of high levels of
emigration, which originated in the nineteenth century as a result
of poverty and famine.

Successive failures of potato crops produced hardship in many
parts of Europe during the nineteenth century: the water mould
Phytophthora infestans occurs in humid regions with temperatures
ranging between 4 and 29 °C (40 and 80 °F), and infected plants may
rot within two weeks. Oats and dairy produce had traditionally
featured in the diet of tenant farmers along Ireland's Atlantic
seaboard but by the mid-1800s oats had become a cash crop to pay
rents to their landlords, and cows were increasingly beyond their
means.

Potatoes are traditionally grown in ridges made by turning over sods.

Forced into dependence on the cheap and easily grown potato, they faced famine when the blight struck. Because of a range of established political, social and economic policies, the British government's responses were slow and ineffectual and between 1845 and 1852 there was a period of mass starvation, disease, and evictions of families unable to pay rents.

This took place in the midst of relative plenty, as grain and other foodstuffs continued to be grown, produced and exported, mainly to England. One outcome was the beginning of a culture of emigration, which reduced the population of Ireland at the time by 20 to 25 per cent, and continued as a steady drain on the country well into the twentieth century. Approximately a million people died in what was known as the Great Famine and is here called *An Gorta Mór*. Over a million others left the country, largely bound for the US. Many who survived the journey and thrived overseas sent passage money home to siblings, and to parents and grandparents who now lacked community and family structures to support them in their old age.

Rural Ireland retains a race memory of the famine years – which some older people still find it hard to speak about – and the spectre

LEFT: Boiler from a nineteenth-century famine-relief soup kitchen, displayed in the museum in Ballyferriter.

BELOW: Emigration left many buildings in ruins.

of emigration has never really gone away. Towards the beginning of the twenty-first century, confidence generated by the boom years of the Celtic Tiger produced a climate of optimism, but the subsequent economic crash, from which the country has since begun to recover, resulted in a new generation of young people seeking work abroad. At the western end of the Dingle Peninsula part-time work is not hard to find during the tourist season but in order to produce a robust year-round local economy, investment and enterprise are vital. The availability of full-time work and diverse and viable career prospects makes a significant difference in relatively isolated communities where the balance of sustainability can turn on the presence or absence of a handful of families in a village, or the closing of a business or a shop.

Beyond Milltown Bridge, is a large building that was once a sawmill and, since 2012, has been home to The Dingle Whiskey Distillery. The distillery was the brainchild of the late Oliver Hughes whose Porterhouse Brewing Company opened Ireland's first brewpub in Dublin in 1996, spearing the country's thriving craft-brewing movement. His twin inspirations for the distillery were his passion for the complex, creative craft of distilling spirits and his deep love of the area. In 2016 Hughes died suddenly of a heart attack at the age of fifty-seven.

The old mill wheel behind the site of the Dingle Whiskey Distillery.

Mary Ferriter

Mary Ferriter, who manages The Dingle Whiskey Distillery, likens Oliver Hughes to a farmer: 'he ploughed the field and set the seed here but he was gone before the harvest.' The effect of the eleven jobs created in Dingle town by the distillery equates to about a hundred in Killarney, she says: 'and that would be the same as maybe two hundred jobs in Dublin. Growing a business like this here means that, when they leave school, more young people can have the option to build lives and careers at home.

❝ I was educated in Coláiste Íde, the Irish-language boarding school just down the road from the distillery. My father was a Dingle man born into a fishing family, and he and his brothers fished all the way up the Atlantic coast. They ended up in Donegal and that's where I was born. There's a great sense of connectivity along the western seaboard, and a sense of connection between the fishermen here and elsewhere in Europe. Generations back, there's Spanish blood in my own family because the fishing, and even the wrecks that left people stranded here, led to intermarriage.

Fishing's a hard life and it's the same with the farming. People in the west depend on each other, and there's a lot of mutual support. My father always told the story of how he borrowed ten shillings to get him over to London, to find work. He hadn't the price of the passage. But six months later, when he came back after working on the ships in England, he was able to put the ten shillings back in the hand of the woman that lent it to him.

I'd say he might have been fourteen years old when he made that first journey. People here have always raised their children to be self-sufficient because you're raising them knowing they might have to go away. But you hope they'll come back. And I

The copper stills are the heart of the distillery. As well as whiskey, the distillery produces gin and vodka, which are also available internationally.

believe that it's good for them to go, because they learn that there's so much more out there, and bring back new ways of problem-solving, and ways of looking at life. As an employer, I find that's pure gold. That and the work-ethic.

Oliver and his wife, Helen, first came to Dingle from Dublin as students in the 1980s, and they were both in love with this place. And over the years, with his businesses in Dublin and London and New York, he was driving towards this vision. Oliver was a man who worked entirely on instinct. An idea would fire him, or a place would inspire him, and then he'd just go for it. He'd be way ahead of everyone else, and it was only afterwards he'd be able to explain it – it was only when it was done that he knew what it meant.

Like, for us at the distillery, one of the key things we've come to recognise is that we don't make whiskey. Nature does. This place has wonderful spring water and, because timber is an organic material, each individual barrel will have an individual effect on the spirit that's matured in it. And then we have the Gulf Stream that affords us this soft climate. During the ageing process of whiskey a loss happens because of evaporation through the cask – when a cask is opened you'd expect to find you'd lost around two per cent of the alcohol in the first year and one per cent a year thereafter, and that's called "the angels' share". Now there's been no distillery documented here before, so we weren't aware of how the Dingle climate would affect the angels' share in our case, but our first cask was filled at a strength of 63.5 on 18 December 2012, and when that cask was opened on 19 December 2015, the strength was 60.8. So the angels were good.

Oliver used to say that his vision for the distillery was about more than just making whiskey. It was about making it here, in Dingle, with everything that implied. And that's something we're very aware of. People who come to live or set up business here must do their homework ahead. They must understand that local people want to protect our culture and the Irish language and that that's something you have to respect and take into account. Everyone has to accept a share in the responsibility for preserving what's here. It applies to us in the distillery, for example, when it comes to processes we're introducing that might not be expressed by words already in use in the Irish language – say something like 'triple distilling'. Now, the labels on our bottles would be in both English and in Irish, and we're going to local sources and translators to establish and confirm the terminology in Irish. And we find that the people who invest in our product – our Founding Fathers, say, whose names are on our first casks – they respect that sense that the product belongs to the place. I think they're drawn to the distillery because they recognise that sense of belonging, and they tell me it's something they want to be part of and share.

Oliver Hughes (l) and his son Elliot (r) with Cormac O'Connor, a member of staff, and Mary Ferriter.

As an employer I'd see people come in who might have degrees, but they don't have what I call the life skills, the common sense to apply to a job, and those are the qualities you need in a modern marketplace. West Kerry people have that adaptability and they're able to think on their feet. Half the time I don't think they're even aware of it. It's just how they are and it's how they've always been. We're shaped by the sea and the land and the way they affect us, but we're also shaped by our history and the hard times.

Oliver ploughed forward with his vision for the distillery and we're rooted deep here now. There have been mills on this site for centuries and as late as 1978 the mill wheel was still turning. You want to keep that sense of history in the place. What happens from generation to generation is just another turn of the wheel. ⌐

Whiskey barrels in the distillery.

Milltown is the starting point for the Slea Head Drive, a circular route that forms part of the Wild Atlantic Way. For some visitors the drive is an opportunity to see some of the most stunning sites on the peninsula from a coach or a car window, to stop at places designated as particularly good for taking photographs, and then to return for a browse through the town's shops or the next meal. For others who are willing to stop and take things more slowly, it offers a window on a unique and ancient cultural inheritance preserved in a contemporary setting, and an opportunity to explore and consider the nuances of Irish identity.

Beyond Milltown Bridge, the Slea Head Drive takes you through an area that surrounded the seat of Lord Ventry, the landlord whose family once held control over most of the Dingle Peninsula. Like many Anglo-Irish landowners, he claimed descent from settlers who came to Ireland during the twelfth-century Norman invasion. His residence, Burnham House, surrounded by 104 acres of estate, including 50 acres of woodland, was built in 1790. In order to establish and improve his estate, Lord Ventry evicted the local population of farmers and fishermen and relocated them to other parts of the area, including Cooleen in Dingle town and to land as far away as Castlegregory on the eastern side of Mount Brandon. In 1922, after at least 400 years in the area, the family sold off the estate and returned to England and in 1927 Burnham House became the Irish-language boarding school Coláiste Íde.

Former estates of this kind can be seen all over Ireland. Besides the house itself, which is not open to visitors, the most obvious indicators of Lord Ventry's presence in Burnham are the surrounding woodland and the small houses and old forge that line the roadside. Built to accommodate estate workers, the houses and the forge incorporate dressed stone and share design features that are not native to the area. The forge now houses a stone workshop and sculpture gallery. In an interview given in 2002 to the newspaper *Kerry's Eye*, Jim de Barra, the last blacksmith to work the forge, remembered his childhood. 'I learned my trade ... from my father. He did a lot of horseshoes, and for the estate here for the Ventrys he did gates and railings. By the time I reached ten years of age the Ventrys were gone.'

Hillside farms west of Dingle.

The story of the local landlord's long period of control and eventual departure is repeated in other stories all over Ireland. After the Great Famine the power of the landlords began to be threatened by a series of political movements which, along with the subsequent War of Independence (1919–1921), ultimately unseated them. The process of returning land to the native population required a series of Land Acts introduced by the British government between 1870 and 1909 and by the Irish government after the period of civil war (1922–1923) that followed the War of Independence.

The initial nineteenth-century Land Acts attempted to reconcile the tenants to the existing system by offering concessions such as fixity of tenure and fair rent review, alongside loans for those who wished to buy out their holdings. But by the end of the period of transfer the majority of landlords had been compensated for what was effectively the compulsory acquisition of their estates. The government money provided for compensation was paid back up to and during the establishment of Ireland's independence, and offset against other concessions afterwards. This process was acrimonious and complex and, ten years after the treaty which ended Ireland's War of Independence, led to the imposition of unilateral trade restrictions by both countries in an economic war with Britain that lasted until 1938, severely damaging the newly independent state's economy.

The dressed-stone wall of the forge in Burnham.

'*Bó*', the Irish for 'cow' is also the root of '*bóthar*', which means 'road'.

The landscape that surrounds you as you drive into the west is far more sparsely populated than it was in the nineteenth and early twentieth century, the fields are larger and the style and distribution of the buildings is different. Unlike the more sophisticated buildings near to the former seat of Lord Ventry, nineteenth-century farmhouses were generally constructed of field stones or of lime-washed stone and sod, and had thatched roofs; and up to the early years of the twentieth century they tended to be built in groups of dwellings with adjacent outhouses. The Irish-language word for such a building is *clochán* and in English a 'cloghane' also came to be used for a village. Unlike English villages, cloghanes were collections of dwellings without the presence of shops, a post office or church, or other formal community space. The inhabitants were fishing and farming families whose land was cultivated on the rundale system.

In this system, which existed from the Early Medieval period, buildings were clustered on the best land available, which was tilled, and livestock was grazed in summer on surrounding land of inferior quality: younger members of a community often lived with its sheep and cattle in temporary dwellings on the uplands, a practice known in English as 'transhumance' or 'booleying' (which takes its root *bó* from the Old Irish word for 'cow'). A central element of the system involved ensuring that each family had an equal share of good and

An early twentieth-century two-storey house. Many older dwellings have survived as farm sheds.

poor fields, and that arable land was communally improved and maintained by fertilisation and crop rotation.

By the early decades of the twentieth century, partly as a result of changes arising from the success of the Land War, the rundale system became obsolete. At the same time, with the intention of pacifying political and social unrest in Ireland, the British government initiated rural housing schemes to build new dwellings at greater removes from each other, deeming the quality of the existing housing and the density of habitation to be unhygienic. Many of these single-storey, slate-roofed dwellings, known as 'Congested Districts Board houses' remain recognisable: others, now extended and painted, are less easy for the passer-by to identify. Later on, Irish government schemes provided grants for two-storey houses: those which retain their original unpainted, rendered finish are noticeable features in the landscape. Numbers of the earlier stone dwellings, now roofed in corrugated iron or tar instead of thatch, have become farm outhouses.

During the later twentieth century, ribbon development along the roadsides removed almost all surviving sense of the former *clochán* groupings. More recently, local and national planning policy has reverted to the concept of clustered dwellings as an ideal, and the landscape has been zoned to restrict building and other

development in areas of outstanding natural beauty.

What is remarkable throughout the area west of Dingle is that so much evidence of prehistoric habitation is present in the landscape. At Milltown, in the front garden of a modern guesthouse is a standing stone over 2 metres tall, known locally as 'the milestone'. Dated to 2000–1400 BC, and probably an ancient boundary marker, it has stood in the same location since the Bronze Age, bearing witness to the successive waves of settlers from other parts of Ireland and from abroad, each of which has added to the fascination of the area.

Gallán na Cille Brice is a Bronze Age standing stone located in a guesthouse garden in Milltown.

LORD VENTRY

The title Baron Ventry was created in 1800 by the British Crown and bestowed on Thomas Mullins, a Baronet whose family claimed descent from the Norman de Moleyns family and had long been landlords over the majority of the Dingle Peninsula. Lord Ventry also claimed descent from a family seated at Burnham, Norfolk, in England, hence the name Burnham House (now Coláiste Íde). The area around the house is still called Burnham in English. There is evidence that an earlier residence belonging to the same family once occupied the site, called Ballingolin Castle and named after a nearby village.

Until the late nineteenth century the majority of land in Ireland was owned by Anglo-Irish nobility or gentry to whom it had been granted or sold over almost seven centuries of English colonisation since the Norman invasion. With the passage of time the native aristocracy had either been killed or driven out, and the peasantry had become tenant farmers on large estates. The estates were often owned by absentee landlords and run by agents who were either native Irishmen or had been imported from the owners' English estates. Tenants were regularly subjected to crippling rent increases, known as rack-renting, and forced evictions. Eyewitnesses' stories of life under the last Lord Ventry are still remembered by the peninsula's older inhabitants.

From the 1870s rural Ireland was gripped by three decades of agrarian agitation, now known as the Land War. It was coordinated by the Irish National Land League, which was dedicated to bettering the position of Ireland's tenant farmers and to a redistribution of land to tenants from landlords, especially absentees.

The Land League, founded in 1879, elected Charles Stewart Parnell as its president. Despite internal division – and after much hardship endured by a rural population that had already been decimated by the famine and sickness caused by potato blight earlier in the century – its aims were broadly achieved. This success fuelled Ireland's cultural revival, which, in turn, inspired a renewed sense of nationalism and fed into the movements which led to Ireland's 1916 Rising and subsequent War of Independence.

The woods surrounding the former Burnham House. Cruach Mhárthain is in the distance.

3 Ventry

Ventry viewed from the old pier at Cuan.

CORCA DHUIBHNE, the Irish-language name for the Dingle Peninsula, means 'the territory of the people of Danu (or Duibhne)'. Danu, whose name survives across Europe in place names from the Danube to the Don, was a fertility goddess of the ancient Celts, primarily associated with water; female deities with the same characteristics can be found in early Indo-European societies from Corca Dhuibhne to northern India. The origins of the people known as the Corcu Duibhne, who were early inhabitants of the Dingle and adjacent Iveragh peninsulas, are unknown. Danu's name, in its Latin form 'Dovinia', appears in Burnham and Com Dhíneoil (Coumeenole), for example, on stones apparently used as grave and boundary markers. A carving depicting a concentric spiral, the symbol of the goddess, was discovered here in 2011 on a medieval pilgrimage route, *Cosán na Naomh* (The Saint's Path). Potentially dating to the Bronze Age (*c* 2500 – 500 BC), the rock art suggests that Early Christian society in the area subsumed, and for a period may have co-existed with, earlier pagan ritual.

When speaking English, the Irish language is referred to as 'Irish', not 'Gaelic'. In Irish it's referred to as *'Gaeilge'*, which in the dialect used in Munster is pronounced *'Gwale-'n'*. The language has three distinct dialects – usually referred to as Ulster, Connacht and Munster Irish – and flourishes primarily along the Atlantic seaboard in what are known as Gaeltacht areas. Within living memory there were native Irish speakers who had little or no English. Today, everyone raised in a Gaeltacht has fluent English as well as speaking Irish as a first language. Munster's principal Gaeltacht is here at the western end of the Dingle Peninsula, and the farther west you travel the more Irish you'll see and hear; the heartland can be found back west, beyond Dingle town.

Although Irish is the official first language of the Republic, for the majority of Irish citizens it's just a subject learned in school. In Gaeltacht areas it is the language of everyday life. The detailed picture, however, is more complex. Many people who have learnt their Irish in school choose to speak it regularly, and some families from non-Gaeltacht areas raise and educate their children entirely through Irish. These *Gaeilgeoirí,* an expanding and largely urban population of uncertain size, have a vital role in the continuing survival of the language: according to the 2011 Republic of Ireland

Evening on Ventry strand.

census 77,185 people speak Irish daily outside the education system, a figure that includes 23,175 people in Gaeltacht areas who speak it as their first language.

As you travel on from Burnham, public signage gives the most immediate signal that this is the heart of the Gaeltacht. Road and other signs throughout Ireland appear both in Irish and English but here you will commonly see untranslated Irish names, signs and posters on shops, community halls and churches, and school buildings. It's worth knowing that while speed limits are indicated on signs in kilometres the people you talk to may describe distances either in kilometres or miles.

Travelling into the countryside it is important to remember that roads here are narrow and should be taken with care. Drivers on the back roads need to be aware of the possible presence of dogs, hens, sheep and cattle. Yellow triangular signs with a black image of a cow and the words 'AINMHITHE AG TRASNÚ', meaning 'animals crossing', indicate points where you may need to wait while livestock is herded between fields and farmyards. The animals are

'Animals Crossing' sign on a back road west of Dingle.

Ceann Trá, or Ventry, post office and strand.

usually driven by someone walking, on a bike or in a car, with a dog working behind them. A signal from the farmer may tell you either to stop your engine and wait at a distance or to continue to drive slowly behind or past them. A wave and a word of thanks will send you on your way again, and the gentle rhythms of the work can be very restful for an onlooker.

The movement of animals is not confined to the points where you see these signs and it is important to be aware that the entire length of the Slea Head Drive takes the visitor through working farmland. It is also important to note that pedestrians use these roads, which have no sidewalks, footpaths or pavements. If you're driving, slow down when you pass a walker. If you're walking, walk facing the oncoming traffic and step back as close as you can to the wall or the ditch to allow approaching vehicles to pass you. If you encounter individuals or groups on horseback, take the same precautions. Meeting an oncomer's eyes and raising a hand or a finger in salute isn't just an act of courtesy, it's also conducive to road safety.

While there are only two hotels west of Dingle town, the standards of accommodation in small B&Bs and guesthouses in the west end of the peninsula are high: bedrooms will almost always be en suite, food will be home-cooked and, if evening meals aren't served, your hosts will always be willing to provide suggestions about where to eat locally, as well as information about the locality and what's happening nearby during your stay. Many of the B&Bs are run by families who first opened their homes to visitors a generation ago, to take in students of Irish. In some cases hospitality has now become a primary source of summer income, in others, your hostess will be the *bean an tigh* (woman of the house) in a family home, a working farmhouse or perhaps a pub. There's no better way to get to know the end of the peninsula than to spend at least a few nights back west; and if you want to move on from one place and explore another, your hosts will often be able to make recommendations and even to phone ahead for you, to check availability. There are also many purpose-built holiday cottages to rent, and older houses renovated for the purpose of short-term letting.

The route of the Slea Head Drive from Burnham to the seaside village of Ventry takes you between farmland and the ocean. The name 'Ventry' is an anglicisation of *Ceann Trá* or *Fionn Trá*, which translates either as 'The Head of the Strand' or 'The Fair Strand'. The village overlooks the long, curving beach backed by low sand dunes. At this end of the beach is a small pier and, above it, a cluster of

At the south end of Ventry strand.

dwellings and holiday cottages, a pub and a post office. Across the road from the post office, which is also a general shop, is a single-storey building surrounded by a schoolyard. One of seven national (primary) schools serving the community back west, it currently employs three staff members.

Unusually for the area, there are two triangular expanses of grass at the junction of the roads outside the pub, producing the effect of a miniature version of an English village green. In 2016, a bench in memory of The O'Rahilly, a north Kerry-born hero of Ireland's 1916 Rising, was erected here. One of the founder members of the nationalist Irish Volunteers, The O'Rahilly, who was the organisation's Director of Arms, helped west Kerry men to arm and train in the run-up to the rising. His wife Nancy (Nannie), an American and a founder member in 1914 of the women's nationalist organisation *Cumann na mBan*, is also named on the memorial. Having begun their married life in the USA and returned to Ireland in 1909, the O'Rahillys regularly came to Corca Dhuibhne to study Irish: the house they owned in the Ventry area is still in the possession of the family. After attempting to halt the 1916 Rising when British interception of German guns that were to have been landed on the Kerry coast made its failure inevitable, The O'Rahilly joined the rebel headquarters in the General Post Office in Dublin. He was killed leading an action to cover the retreat from the burning building. For some time after her husband's death Nannie continued to be active in politics and, at one point, was arrested along with her young family. She resigned from her position as a Vice-President of Cumann na mBan in 1922, during the civil war that followed Ireland's War of Independence, and died in Dublin in 1961.

The Republic of Ireland maintained neutrality during the Second World War. On the reverse of a stone on Ventry green giving the name of the village is an inscription commemorating a 'magnanimous action' taken on 4 October 1939 by the captain of a German U-boat. Having sunk the Greek merchant ship *Diamantis* off England's Cornish coast, *U-35* picked up the ship's surviving crew members and took the considerable risk of landing them here.

CONVERSATION:
Séamas Ó Luing

Postmaster Séamas Ó Luing's family has served the community in Ceann Trá for generations.

❝ There was a time, in the 1970s, when there were still local shops selling provisions in every village back here, and you wouldn't have far to go to a petrol pump or a post office. And what's here today is still all about community and local enterprise. If you go into a café, say, the chances are that the scones you'll get with your tea or your coffee will be home-baked. And you certainly won't find a Starbucks or a McDonalds. But if a shopkeeper retires or moves on there's always a likelihood that the service will go, and even if a place is only closed for a while, it's a break in continuity. At the end of the day it's a case of use it or lose it.

I'm deeply involved in the Irish Postmasters' Union and as far back as I remember it's been the same. In the 1980s/90s, when the network of post offices nationwide numbered 1,800, rural communities were fighting off a plan to reduce it to something

A signpost by the green in Ventry.

like 600. So the sense of fighting for survival has been ever-present and ongoing. But, having said that, there's a real sense of positivity about the amount of network we've held on to, and about the future. Usually whatever happens in the UK gets imported in here to Ireland, but now they've seen the damage they've done to the towns and villages and post office network over there, and they've tried to reverse it or to hold it back, and to pay a subsidy to maintain a post office as the last link in a social network that's been destroyed. Ireland has made losses that are non-reversible too but, all the same, we're hanging on and still fighting, and we can point to other countries to show what happens if you don't.

We're a small country and we've got direct access to local politicians and I think that in the last election people realised how important rural affairs are in terms of the social cohesion of the country as a whole. What do we want and where do we want to live? What kind of services do we want to have in the areas we want to live in? What kind of place do we want for ourselves and, round these parts, what kind of place do tourists want to visit?

There's always been a history here of tourism based on language, culture and people. The danger now is that if government policy isn't progressive enough to make sure that local people can live here, then the very things that draw visitors in will be eroded. Planning is a big issue, in terms of people getting permission to build in their own area. And it's important that visitors have a chance to engage with the people here as well as taking photos of the stunning scenery. What we want is a sustainable tourist industry which isn't just about the numbers of people who come here but the quality of the experience they get.

Being able to shop locally is a big thing. I've ledgers for this shop here in my family that go back to the late 1800s. My great-grandfather was a cooper, so he made barrels, which was a big trade up to the 1920s and 1930s, and I remember selling paraffin out of the barrel before the rural electrification scheme took off: even after the electric light came in the 1960s and 1970s people still used paraffin lamps and heaters and you'd sell them oil from the barrel. Now the shop offers Internet access and we have a deli counter and takeaway teas and coffees, but I'm still selling ordinary provisions and household staples, and fuel for fires. People don't want to have to travel miles for a litre of milk or a loaf of bread. And a post office or a shop wouldn't just be a place to post a parcel or to buy something, it'd be a focal point where local people meet and interact.

You'd have a big sense of community in the villages. Communities came together and fundraised to build the halls, say, and then later, when the original buildings mightn't have been fit for purpose any more, they'd come together again, raise their own funds, apply to the authorities for matching funding, and a new hall was built. They'd be used for all sorts. Meetings and shows, and the schools would use them. They'd be here for everyone.

Déantar gnó anseo trí Ghaeilge

ABOVE: 'Business is done here through Irish' sign in the post office in Ceann Trá.

LEFT: The Community Hall.

LEFT: Ceann Trá national school.

Sand dunes on Ventry strand.

'The use of the language has changed in my lifetime. Actually, I think there's probably more people speaking it now than spoke it at one time, but they'd be bilingual now so more English words and phrases are used, so it's not pure the way it was. And that's sad because the old people had a beautiful use of the language. But there are so many young people now wanting to speak it, and families where Irish is what children hear from the day they're born. There's a lot of hope for the language. And there's a big danger in crying wolf, because a negative attitude becomes a self-fulfilling prophecy.

Like hundreds of other indigenous languages worldwide, Irish is under constant pressure from the twin beliefs that 'modern' languages are intrinsically superior to 'old' ones and that linguistic diversity has no value in a world driven by the demands of a global economy.

But I think now, more than ever, people here believe in the value of the language as part of our cultural inheritance. We're always trying to find new ways of investing in it. And ways to improve how we pass on our culture in schools – things that kids might have learned at home or in the fields in the past are coming to them in the classroom now, which is why local schools are important. Because there are local stories and local music and songs that belong to particular areas, and when kids pick their own up at a young age they have them forever.

Ventry Strand, which curves away below the schoolyard, is the setting of *Cath Finntrágha* (The Battle of Ventry), one of many stories passed on here through generations by word of mouth. It belongs to a cycle that chronicles the exploits of the legendary Fionn Mac Cumhaill and his band of warriors, known as the Fianna. Written references to *Cath Finntrágha* occur as early as the twelfth century and the manuscripts probably contain echoes of older, oral versions.

The story begins when Ireland is threatened by the arrival, at Ventry Strand, of the massed armies of The King of The World, Dáire Donn, who has been led there by Glas Mac Dreamhain, a renegade member of the Fianna. When the invading fleet is seen on the horizon, most of the Fianna are elsewhere. So Conn Crithir, a sentry who has been left on guard, prepares to defend the beach single-handedly. When it comes to it, however, Glas will not fight a former companion, so together they hold the beach until Fionn and the Fianna arrive.

The story involves a series of heroic exploits, fought over an extended period of time and centring on single combat, in the manner of Homer's *Iliad*. While Glas and Conn Crithir are waiting for the others, they are protected by three witches who transform stalks, puffballs and watercress into the appearance of armies, and bring healing water from a spring on the nearby Eagle's Mountain, Sliabh an Iolair.

ABOVE: Ventry Strand at low tide.
RIGHT: Puffballs and Watercress.

Sunset at Ventry Strand.

Interwoven through the story is the tale of Crea, the wife of Caol, a hero of the Fianna. The battle ends with her search for her husband among the piles of dead and wounded littered along the blood-soaked strand. She finds him dead on the shoreline and, lying beside him, praises his courage and laments his loss before dying of a broken heart.

In living memory *Cath Finntrágha* was recited locally at fireside gatherings and – though the elaborate skill of recitation over several nights of consecutive storytelling is now lost – the children who play in the schoolyard above Ventry Strand today will be the next generation to pass it on.

A sense of communal responsibility is characteristic of life here. Although the rundale system disappeared in the early decades of the twentieth century, the concept of the '*meitheal*' survives. A *meitheal* is a group of neighbours who come together to engage in a task that would be too much for a single individual or family. By this means, the seasonal work of an entire neighbourhood could be addressed collectively, making the most of the good weather and the time available. In recent times the idea of the *meitheal* has been expressed more formally in community organisations working with

The fields above Ventry, being south-facing, receive maximum year-round sunlight.

government and local government schemes for social development; but the underlying culture continues to permeate day-to-day life, and the fundraising for the halls is representative of many social, educational and tourist initiatives that emerge locally.

Established in 1980, Údarás na Gaeltachta is Ireland's regional authority responsible for the economic, social and cultural development of the country's Gaeltacht areas. Its offices in Kerry are situated in Dingle, in an eye-catching building near Milltown Bridge. The authority's overall objective is to ensure that Irish remains the primary language of the Gaeltacht and is passed on to future generations. Working in association with other government and local bodies, it funds and fosters a wide range of enterprise-development and job-creation initiatives and supports strategic language, cultural and community-based activities.

The peninsula's co-operative development organisation, Comharchumann Forbartha Chorca Dhuibhne was established in 1967, to enhance the social, economic and cultural life of the community. Currently funded by a number of government departments and bodies, including Údarás na Gaeltachta and The Arts Council, its initial emphasis was on directing local and national government attention to the needs of the area's farmers and fishermen. In the 1970s its scope increased to include the educational sector, which is now its main focus. Coláistí Chorca Dhuibhne, a subsidiary of the Comharchumann, organises courses at primary and secondary school level in the Irish language. (http://www.colaiste.ie/). Oidhreacht Chorca Dhuibhne, another subsidiary, initiates cultural activities and Irish courses for adults. (http://www.oidhreacht.ie/). 'Oidhreacht' is the Irish word for 'heritage'.

Continuing along the road from the post office for about two miles you come to Ard a' Bhóthair, (The Top of the Road). Here, at the four corners of a crossroads, are a house once used by a nineteenth-century US folklorist, a shop and a pub owned by the family of the late Gaelic football hero, Páidí Ó Sé, and Ventry parish church.

The nineteenth-century Catholic church is dedicated to the fourth-century martyr Catherine of Alexandria who probably never existed outside folklore.

The reason for her veneration in this remote part of west Kerry is unknown, although she appears to have been invoked in medieval Europe as a protector of seafarers, which may account for it. The feast of St Caitlín, as she is known in the area, takes place on 25 November. It is celebrated with music and other cultural events, and visits are made to the local graveyard where the medieval parish church was situated.

The nineteenth-century Catholic church in Ventry.

Erected in 2015, the bronze statue of Páidí Ó Sé, by sculptor Seamus Connolly, is mounted on Valentia Island slate.

Outside Páidí Ó Sé's pub is a statue of the football hero. Inside, the pub has a big-screen TV area and is decorated with sporting and celebrity memorabilia. Traditional music sessions are also frequently held there. A native of Ventry, with eight All-Ireland wins to his name as a player and two as a manager, between the 1970s and the 2000s, Ó Sé was one of the most decorated names in the sport and one of the most recognisable faces in Ireland. The evening after his sudden death in 2012 at the age of fifty-seven, tributes were paid to him at the BBC Sports Personality of the Year awards ceremony, and messages of sympathy to his family were delivered from all over the world.

Jeremiah Curtin, an American who collected and published Native American and Slavic as well as Irish material, visited the area in 1887 and wrote afterwards of 'the peculiar condition of myth tales in Ireland, so well preserved where the Gaelic language is still living, and swept away completely where the language has perished ... The character and mould of a nation's thought are found in its language as nowhere else, and the position of a nation in the scale of humanity is determined irrevocably by its thought'. Curtin's *Myths and Folk-Lore of Ireland*, published in 1890, contains much material collected while staying in Ventry. His own boyhood home, on the Trimborn Farm estate in Greendale, Wisconsin, is listed on the US National Register of Historic Places and owned by the Milwaukee County Historical Society.

Ventry Harbour viewed from The Clasach, with the Iveragh Peninsula beyond.

The turn to the right between the shop and the house stayed in by Jeremiah Curtin takes you up through An Clasach – also known as Mám Clasach and, in English, The Clasach – the high pass that leads between Cruach Mhárthain and Sliabh an Iolair, the last two mountains in the peninsula's rocky spine before it dips into the Atlantic at Dún Chaoin (Dunquin). The turn to the left between the church and the pub leads down to a car park by a graveyard and another stretch of Ventry Strand. On a nearby promontory overlooking the beach and the ocean is the site traditionally known as the grave of Crea and her husband Caol, the last of the Fianna to die in *Cath Finntrágha*.

THE IRISH LANGUAGE

Irish belongs to the Indo-European family of languages spoken over the greater part of Europe and Asia as far as northern India: the Romance languages, evolved from Vulgar Latin between the sixth and ninth centuries, form a relatively modern branch within the family. Latin had no significant effect on Irish until the coming of Christianity in the fourth century and its presence derives largely from Christian terminology. There are Old, Middle and Modern forms of Irish, as in English, and standardised spelling and grammar were introduced in 1958. Because standardisation happened recently and the native culture is essentially an oral one, vernacular pronunciation, spelling and grammar survive and thrive.

The old script, variations of which you'll occasionally see on signs and souvenirs, is no longer taught in schools. Today, printed Irish, like English, uses Roman typefaces, though the Irish alphabet doesn't include the letters j, k, q, v, w, x, y or z. Accented vowels indicate a lengthened sound – for example the ú sound in the word *Dún*, which means fort, is pronounced as 'oo'. The form of a noun varies according to case, the genitive being noticeable on road signs – the word *Bóthar*, 'Road', for example, becomes *Ard a' Bhóthair* in the place name that translates as 'the top of the road'.

The history of the language has been shaped by evolving politics and policies over almost eight centuries of British and post-colonial rule. As in many colonised countries, the first English settlers considered the indigenous language barbaric. Later, though many Irish-language scholars came from the largely Protestant Anglo-Irish gentry, Irish came to be associated with Catholicism, sedition, and the 'uneducated' rural poor.

By the eighteenth century Roman Catholic schools were outlawed, as part of an attempt to force all British subjects to conform to Anglicanism. Many wealthy Irish families chose to educate their children at Catholic schools and colleges in mainland Europe, while 'hedge schools' at home taught the rural poor. Theoretically illegal and sometimes literally held under hedgerows, these schools continued an ancient, mainly oral, process of education, through Irish.

In 1831, the British government set up national schools in Ireland. It aimed to 'unite in one system children of different creeds' and to ensure that they spoke English. The underlying egalitarian ethos was laudable, as was the attempt to offer universal education, but the negative effects on the native language were significant. Children wore 'tally sticks' and were beaten according to the number of the notches that were added to the stick each time they were heard speaking Irish. Parents often cooperated, afraid that Irish would hinder their children's prospects if they emigrated. That fear persisted here within living memory, alongside a dogged determination to preserve a language that was seen as a precious inheritance.

At the end of the nineteenth century and the beginning of the twentieth century, Irish began to be taught both in schools and by nationalist and cultural revival groups. When an independent state was established in 1922, Irish was confirmed as its official language, and in 2007 it became an official and working language of the European Union.

Signage in Irish in Ventry.

4 Around Slea Head

Approaching Dún Mór from Ventry, on the Slea Head Drive.

Slea Head from the north.

Southern slopes of Mount Eagle.

'**S**LEA HEAD', is an Anglicisation of the Irish '*Ceann Sléibhe*' ('the head of the mountain'). The Slea Head Drive now curves round the high bulk of Sliabh an Iolair, the eagle's mountain from which the witches brought healing water in the story of the Battle of Ventry. The section that stretches out to Slea Head itself was started as a famine-relief project in 1845; in the year in which it began, a workman and his wife, who had brought him food, were killed when a rock under which they were sheltering fell on them. Construction was suspended when a change in policy resulted in the destitute having to give up their homes and enter the

A curve in the road on the Slea Head Drive near Fahan.

Poor House in Dingle rather than work for assistance: the road-building was eventually completed in 1895.

Most of this part of the road clings to the cliff edge and has spectacular views of the ocean, the Blasket Islands and the rugged coastline farther west. It also gives access to a series of dramatic archaeological sites. *An Dún Beag* (The Little Fort) is an Iron Age or possibly Early Christian promontory fort. The site has suffered significant erosion since it was first recorded in the early nineteenth century. In 1977 the Office of Public Works initiated an excavation to try to reveal its chronology and the nature of its occupational sequence before it was further destroyed. It was found to have been defended by lines of earthen banks, trenches and an inner drystone rampart with a complex entrance flanked by two guard-chambers. A souterrain (underground passage) extends under the causeway from this entrance and in the interior is a single stone hut. The inner stone rampart extends across the promontory for 29 metres. This is only about half the length recorded in 1856: much of the western half has fallen into the ocean. The fort appears to have had two construction phases and two major phases of occupation, during which wooden structures may have been erected within the stone defences. Neither period seems to have lasted for

ABOVE: Christian cross,
Fahan Group.

TOP RIGHT: An Dún Beag
promontory fort.

RIGHT: Beehive huts of the
Fahan Group.

any great length of time and it is possible that it was only occupied at times of emergency. The bones of birds, fish, sheep, pig and deer were recovered, and clusters of stake holes probably indicate the presence of tripods for supporting cooking vessels over fires. Along the length of one of the defensive ditches are indications of a wattle fence. A charcoal layer, possibly resulting from the burning of this fence, produced a radiocarbon date of about 580 BC. In January 2014, during a severe storm, a further portion of the fort was lost to the Atlantic. The rest of the site survives and is well worth a visit.

Five interconnected beehive huts are located to the landward side as you travel on towards Slea Head. They were built without mortar in a method known as corbelling in which successive circles of stone, each a little closer to the centre than the one beneath, rise to a small aperture at the top, which has a capstone. Corbelling was used as a building method in Ireland as early as 3100 BC and as recently as

ABOVE: The approach to Slea Head with its views of the Blasket Islands.

BELOW: The crucifix by the road at Slea Head.

the 1950s. These structures have been dated to the twelfth century, but may be older and their use may have changed over time.

So many huts of this kind, known as the Fahan Group, have been identified on this southern slope of Sliabh an Iolair, that in his work *On an ancient settlement in the south-west of the Barony of Korkaguiney, Kerry* the archaeologist R. A. S. Macalister, professor of Celtic Archaeology in University College Dublin from 1909 to 1943, referred to them as 'the City of Fahan'.

They may have been single family dwellings or, as suggested in Peter Harbison's book *Pilgrimage in Ireland* (Syracuse University Press, 1992), accommodation for pilgrims either arriving by sea from the south to take part in the medieval pilgrimage to the top of Mount Brandon, or continuing on the next stage of a western maritime pilgrimage.

As you approach the end of the peninsula the road narrows, and at one corner a stream tumbles down the mountain, spreads across the road, and spills down the cliff face to the ocean. From about this point until you turn inland again beyond Slea Head, you are on a single-track road with passing places: so go gently, look ahead as far as you can, and keep a good distance from the vehicle in front to allow space for reversing. Some of the buildings you pass are holiday homes but others are farms, which, in some cases, offer bed and breakfast to visitors.

Slea Head itself, marked on the road by a large, white crucifixion scene, offers stunning views eastwards to the expanse of Dingle Bay and south and south-west to Valentia and Skellig Michael, islands off the adjacent Iveragh Peninsula. In 1866, the first transatlantic cable, which continued in use until 1965, was laid from Valentia Island to Canada's Newfoundland. To the north-west is Dún Mór Head (*Doon More* – The Big Fort), the most westerly point in mainland Europe. Directly to your west is the Great Blasket island, the largest of the group of islands that emerges from the Atlantic Ocean as the continuation of the Dingle Peninsula's ancient rocky spine. The dwindling community that lived on the islands was officially evacuated with government assistance in the 1950s, and the group is now uninhabited. Information about boat trips to the Great Blasket, which run in summer from various points in Dingle and back west, can be had locally and from the tourist office in Dingle.

Jimmy Hand

Jimmy Hand was born in Kinard, to the east of Dingle, and he, his wife Maria Sullivan of An Baile Uachtarach (The Upper Town) and their young family now live in a house they built back west. As well as working with his brother as a fisherman, Jimmy has worked on the boat trips to the Great Blasket island and as a diver.

❝ My great grandfather, his name was Peter Hand, he was in the British Navy and he was stationed in Dingle. That's where the salt water came from in my family. My mother's nickname was Bob and they called her 'Bob The Bottle' because of a message in a bottle she found on a beach. It was written by a GI, a Yank going back to America after the Second World War, and she found it and his address was in it and she wrote to him. And in the end he came over to meet her. She got a taxi into Tralee and she met him and he wanted to marry her. But she wouldn't. There was too much press round when she got there, they were all looking for the story. She wasn't interested in all that so she came home again and she married my father. One of my brothers still has the bottle, a little small brown one you'd get aspirins in.

My father used to have a small fishing boat and I started roughly when I was about ten and I've been fishing since. From there me and a brother of mine, Seán, bought a boat and we had others after it. My brother Tom does the eco-marine tours. And Seán started diving in 1982 and we'd work at that together too. One thing led to another and during the boom, I suppose, we were servicing thirty-six moorings a year. That was a heap of work.

A diver working on boats in Dingle.

The bottom line is that fishing's about the weather. Since I've started, no two years are alike. Ever from day one. We've always kept a log and every single year is totally different and varied. You might get five or six bad years back to back and then it'll come good again. I even have a clip in there of a 1935 newspaper and it says mackerel stocks in Dingle are running out. And we're still drawing today. It's like the language, they're always saying it's finished and it never is. Even when the first trawler with an engine came to Dingle they destroyed the engine with sledge-hammers. They said the engines would wipe out fishing. Well, engines have got bigger and the fishing is still pretty much the same.

But in the last ten years, if you count the days on your hand, there's maybe three years of it that were proper good, in terms of the weather. And then you've a combination of prices, demand and all this craic. Price of fish goes up. Price of oil goes down. When I started fishing first, diesel was 12 cents a litre, it was the last thought in your mind. Now fuel is 86 cents. When we started out first we used make our own lobster pots – out of wire and whatever, and we tried twig pots one year. You only required about a hundred to make a living out of it. It wasn't that you were catching massive amounts of fish, but your expenses were low. In 1986/87 we were getting £4.50 per lb for lobster. If you work

Fishing boats moored in Dingle Harbour.

that out now it would be about €27 or €28 a kilo in today's money. And these days they're only getting €17 or €18 a kilo. So the scale has tipped in the wrong direction for now.

The funny thing about fishing is every generation thinks it can do it better than the one before – "I can go farther, I can work harder, I can catch more fish." Now we have better gear and technology, the systems are different so there'd be half the lifting, maybe, and you can haul more pots. But it still comes down to the same thing. Days at sea. You've got so many hours of daylight in the day. You can haul so many pots in a day. You can only catch so many fish in a day. Unless you get to the big super-trawlers, when they come in with two crews and work twenty-four hours a day and they're just like a hoover. But as for fishing here, you'll always hear of some new guy and it's "he landed a hundred boxes of crab yesterday". And you say "what did he do the other 364 days?" The truth is that it seems to balance itself out.

They've improved the design of pots. Long ago they were a French design, they were made of twigs, long, flexible bits of willow. Very good pots but you had to haul them every two or three hours or, when they'd be full, the lobster would get out. Whereas now they have them made of net and when he goes in the pot closes behind him. You can leave that lobster pot for three, four days if you want because he's in and that's that. But, it's funny, the crab will find a way out – if there's any part of a lobster pot that's mended a crab will find it. Even if you mend it with good black twine again, so that it looks exactly the same as the first day, he'll find where the knots are where you mended the hole. And when they find it, they don't really catch it with their claws, they start sawing it with their legs, and when one guy gets tired the next guy moves in and takes over. So if they're left there too long they find where you mended the mesh and they cut through it and every single crab will get out.

'There was a point that fishermen here passed – the difference between fishing for food and fishing to sell. That was back before the middle of the last century. It was the French and Spanish that came round looking to buy and they brought pots – they showed people how to make them and they brought the twigs with them – like bringing kits – and they left them, and then they'd come round again and they'd buy up the catch. Before that it was fishing to eat. The mackerel could be stored in salt and you'd keep it through the winter. Even when I was growing up we ate a hell of a lot of salt mackerel and brown soda bread, so much that I can hardly face them now. And round the shore, people got *bollach*. In English you'd call them wrasse. It's a fish with a skin so tough that a seal wouldn't eat it. They taste very bland but they're easy to catch and the old people loved them, and you can salt them too and keep them in a barrel. They'd go for pollock as well. They'd rather fish close to the shore but at times they'd go farther. They'd go round behind Tiaracht, one of the Blasket Islands, with small nets. In those days they'd be fishing from a *naomhóg*, small boats with a timber frame covered in tarred canvas. And it was dangerous. No communication. They'd have a sail and a crew of oarsmen, no satnav or anything like that. And a *naomhóg* can only take so many fish, and sometimes they'd get a big catch and overload them. Sometimes it was the fish that took them down. These days you couldn't fish from a *naomhóg* for your living even if you wanted to. The regulations wouldn't allow it.

A lot of fishing is being able to read the water. When you're in a small boat you need to know what the tide is and what the wind direction is. You might wait another hour before setting out and that'd make the difference. And it's the same today when we'd be taking boat trips to the island. People don't believe that we can read the swell and we know what's safe and what isn't. It's not just about what you can see on the surface, it's what you know is underneath or even what you know is coming. We'd know the water and the weather round here very well.

When you're taking tourists out you're always aware of the effect on the environment. Like, the boatmen wouldn't want too many people tramping over the island at one time. It can only take so much, like you can only take so much out of the sea without doing harm. You'd want them to take nothing but photos, leave nothing but footprints, because people can damage an environment far quicker than it's able to repair itself. I'd say it's about balance and having basic common sense.

Diving's a wonderful experience. Under the water it's teeming with life and it's gorgeous, just spectacular, totally different to being in a boat. You'd see a whole different world down there face to face. On top of the water you'd see humpback whales, minkes, dolphins, seals, basking sharks. One day back by Tiaracht I found a huge leatherback turtle, big as the table, just swimming on his own. Things have changed in the last while – the water's got warmer. A while back I was watching a pod of fins going through the water and we tried to catch up with them but they were going too fast. It was a pod of killer whales. You'd never see that ten or fifteen years ago. You'd see the odd one, all right, but you'd have to go over and look at it because it was so unusual. Nowadays they're everywhere. The water temperature's rising and it brings a lot of feed. That's bad for fishing because the fish have less interest in bait. They're full to bursting. But it's great for bringing in the big fellows.

The thing about living here is the kids get a great education. They get a great start in the local schools and they learn how to live. There's no better place in the world you can raise kids. What I'd want for my kids is, once they've their Leaving Cert done at school, I'd say don't go to college, go away and find out what you want. Go away for two years. Make it five years. You can't send an eighteen-year-old into college to do what they're going to be doing the rest of their life. They haven't a clue what to do. Say an architectural engineer – how the hell do you know what it means to be an architectural engineer when you're eighteen? That's how I'd advise my girls. They'll do what they do, but that's what I'd advise them. Go and find out what it is that matters to you. What I want for them in life is quality because we're only here for a short time, a very short time altogether. 〞

The western tip of the Dingle Peninsula was more heavily populated in the past. Every strip of viable land was once farmed.

In 1927, after his record-breaking transatlantic flight from New York to Paris, Charles Lindbergh recorded that the first indication of his approach to the European coast was a sea-going fishing vessel. '... closing the throttle as the plane passed within a few feet of the boat I shouted, "Which way is Ireland?" Of course the attempt was useless, and I continued on my course.' There was a heavy mist and he was flying less than 200 feet above the water when he sighted the western end of the Dingle Peninsula. As the single-seat, single-engine monoplane was still out at sea, a thirteen-year-old local boy, called Tomás Ó Cinnéide was receiving the gift of a broken bicycle from his aunt. In his 1982 autobiography *Ar Seachrán*, published in translation in 1997 as *The Wild Rover*, Ó Cinnéide describes walking barefoot home along a beach some miles to the north-east of Slea Head with the bicycle on his shoulder. 'I heard a noise to my right and I looked out towards the mouth of the harbour. Above the Black Rock I saw the bird, as I thought, coming towards me ... What was it only an aeroplane and who was in it only Lindbergh himself coming all on his own from America ... He was directly over my head. I was so delighted that I raised my hand by the way to salute him ...

That is how it was. I was going west and Lindbergh was going east and each one of us was just as happy as the other.'

The social and economic changes that increased exponentially here during the course of the twentieth century began with the arrival of outsiders – including the foreigners seeking to buy fish, described by Jimmy Hand – and with the return of emigrants bringing disposable money. Tomás Ó Cinnéide's autobiography goes on to describe his disappointment when, on reaching home that day in 1927, he tried to repair his broken bicycle. He had to give up because he 'didn't have the parts to put it in working order'. Buying them was out of the question because most families back west at the time had hardly begun to engage with the cash economy.

The beaches below the village of Com Dhíneoil are remarkably beautiful but dangerous for bathing. The name of the village probably comes from Diníl, a local chieftain whose daughter is recorded in medieval *dinnseanchas* as having married the King of Munster. The headland, as its name Dún Mór (Big Fort) suggests, is the site of another promontory fort, though little of the structure survives. An ogham (pronounced *oh-am*) stone with an inscription that includes the partially eroded name 'Dovinia' suggests that the headland may once have been a sanctuary of the goddess Duibhne. Looking north from Dún Mór you can see the site of the schoolhouse that was built as a set for David Lean's film *Ryan's Daughter* (1971).

The two beaches below Coumeenole village.

Ruins of *Ryan's Daughter* schoolhouse.

Much of the film was shot in Com Dhíneoil and the surrounding area, and a whole village was constructed on the side of Cruach Mhárthain above Dún Chaoin, and removed after the shooting. The partially ruined schoolhouse remains in its picturesque setting on the cliffs; it was acquired in the 1980s by the late Tony Ryan, founder of the Ryanair airline, and is still owned by his family.

David Lean's film had a remarkable effect on the western end of the peninsula. Local people still talk about his first visit by helicopter, and the fact that as soon as the production crew arrived in Dingle they went to the local garage and ordered six Land Rovers and six Ford Zephyrs. It was the beginning of what amounted to a turning point in the area's history.

Lean had envisaged that the project would take three months but he and his cast and crew, many imported from Hollywood, were still here fourteen months later. Hold-ups due to bad weather contributed to the expansion of the film's budget from £9 million to £13 million and eventually the production was moved to South Africa, after a long search for a beach that would match the scenes shot locally. Ironically, the unit in Corca Dhuibhne was also

Fibreglass standing stone made for the film *Ryan's Daughter.*

bedevilled by good weather. Niall O'Brien, one of the actors, described how one scene, which required a particularly ferocious storm, extended his original contract of twelve weeks to fifty-two. 'They had a cast and crew on standby for a year while they waited for the big seas.'

The money pumped into local trades and services literally changed lives. Lean's film crew, which had taken over most of the accommodation in Dingle town, rented land for shooting, sourced furniture and props in the area and – besides hiring dozens of local people as extras – employed drivers, caterers and large numbers of tradesmen, such as stonemasons and carpenters, offering prices and wages that were unheard of at the time. The subsequent international success of the film drew attention to the beauty of the area, launching the western end of the peninsula onto the modern tourist market at exactly the time when cheap international travel was becoming more widely available.

After the departure of 'the film people' dramatic stories about the actors and their behaviour continued to circulate and have entered local folklore, from Robert Mitchum creating a mini-marijuana factory in the greenhouse of the house he rented, to Sarah Miles paying a fortune for her cat, flown in from London, to be picked up and driven all the way from Shannon Airport. And, as a monument to Tinsel Town, a large fibreglass cross-inscribed standing stone, a gift from the producers and used as part of the film set, now stands outside Músaem Chorca Dhuibhne, the Museum of the Dingle Peninsula, in nearby Ballyferriter.

BIRDLIFE

Puffins, gulls and birds' eggs formed a significant part of the local diet here in the past and within living memory it was common for people, both on the mainland and the islands, to climb down the cliffs seeking eggs. Birds also had other practical uses: there is a record of the islanders using 'a rush drawn through the oily body of a Stormy Petrel' as a candle.

Now birdwatching is a growing activity on the peninsula with ornithologists and serious 'twitchers' travelling from abroad to watch the thousands of seabirds, waders and duck to be seen locally, and to find rare waders and wildfowl blown across the Atlantic in autumn, and rare gulls in winter.

The peninsula has internationally important island seabird colonies, wetlands and reed beds, harbours and estuaries, sand dunes and coastal cliffs, each with its own special interest. The largest concentration of Chough in north-west Europe breeds here and they are commonly seen around coastal cliffs and pastures. Gannets can be seen throughout the year and Pale-Bellied Brent Geese are regular winter visitors. Black Guillemot breed here; and Hen Harrier, which are almost extinct elsewhere in Ireland, breed in east Kerry and winter in west Kerry, where you can see them quartering low over reed beds. Boat trips around the Blasket Islands provide opportunities to see breeding Auks, Kittiwakes, Puffins and Shearwaters.

Raven, Dipper, Merlin and Curlew can also be observed and, wherever there are trees or other cover, summer visitors and migrants, such as Willow Warbler, Goldcrest, Chiffchaff, Sedge

Herring Gull at Slea Head.

Curlew at An Mhuiríoch.

and Grasshopper Warbler. In the past, one of the most common calls heard here in summer was that of the Corncrake. There are far fewer to be heard nowadays in Ireland, where the Corncrake is on the brink of extinction, but one or two were recorded until recently in overgrown fields on the peninsula's most westerly coastal fringes.

The Irish ornithologist Prof. C. J. Patten, author of *The Aquatic Birds of Great Britain and Ireland* (1906) made two visits to the Dingle Peninsula, in August 1897 and December 1898, but the widely travelled English author H. Seebohm was probably the first ornithologist to visit the Blasket Islands, in September 1856. It is not known whether R. J. Ussher and R. Warren, the Irish authors of *The Birds of Ireland* (1900), went to the Blaskets in person, though their book contains photos of the islands. As late as the 1950s, when S. M. D. Alexander organised an expedition there, the islands were considered fairly inaccessible territory for ornithologists, and the islanders themselves were recognised as the most knowledgeable authorities on the presence and habits of their bird life. According to Alexander, 'We tested them in the case of the Black Guillemot and were shown five nests within a mile of the village on the Great Blasket which we had still not discovered after seven days on that island.'

BirdWatch Ireland has a web page specifically relating to Corca Dhuibhne which is well worth checking for updates (www.birdwatchireland.ie). Visitors with a more casual interest will find boards displaying well-illustrated information at various points around the Slea Head Drive. All birds' eggs are now protected by law, and nests should not be interfered with.

Ringed Plovers and Sanderlings are common waders on the Dingle Peninsula's beaches.

5 Dunquin

Gable of deserted house facing the Atlantic, in Coumeenole, on the approach to Dunquin.

THE DINGLE PENINSULA'S COASTLINE ranges from sandy beaches that change with every tide to high rocky cliffs more resistant to the pounding of the Atlantic Ocean. Yet cliffs, too, are subject to coastal erosion and walkers should always take care. Scrambling out to the farthest possible point to take a selfie may feel fine but the cliff face immediately below may be no more than a ledge of grassy earth and shale suspended above the ocean. It's important never to underestimate the power of the waves, or of the sudden, unexpected gusts of wind, which can be strong enough to lift an adult male off his feet. In 2007, about 1km of the Slea Head Drive had to be reconstructed farther inland following the collapse of the cliff edge after a violent storm and, at Dún Chaoin, during an exceptionally wet winter a few years later, a river of mud swept down from the mountain into the graveyard that stands on the seaward side, above the cliffs.

The stretch of water between the mainland and the Great Blasket is notoriously dangerous to navigate in bad weather. In 1588 two ships of the Spanish Armada foundered here, having taken refuge from the autumn storms. After the Armada's naval defeat by the English, the Spanish ships had tried to make their way home through the North Atlantic. More than twenty were wrecked off the Irish coast, from Antrim, in the north, to the Dingle Peninsula. The first to go down in the Blasket Sound was the *San Juan de Ragusa*.

Houses on the clifftop above Dunquin Pier with the Atlantic Ocean beyond, on a calm day.

Dunmore Head viewed from Dunquin, with Skellig Michael in the distance.

The second, called the *Santa Maria de la Rosa,* dropped anchor, hoping to ride out the storm. But she was driven onto a rock and sank with only one survivor who later testified that, moments before the battered ship went down, the pilot was killed by the captain; an underwater archaeological investigation in 1968 found evidence of desperate last-minute attempts to repair storm damage. A third ship, the *San Juan de Bautista,* which had also entered the Sound, managed to survive and made it back to Spain. Two other vessels, led by the *San Juan de Portugal*, captained by Juan Martínez de Recalde, managed to steer through to calmer water and anchored under the cliffs of the Great Blasket. It was a remarkable piece of seamanship that would probably have been impossible had he not had prior knowledge of the waters: he subsequently brought his ships safely home. Survivors from the wrecks and a reconnaissance party sent out by Recalde were captured by the English and executed in Dingle town.

The spectacular cliffs around Dunquin.

Local people have an innate sense of respect for the power of the ocean, and detailed knowledge of the currents and rocks that surround this end of the peninsula has been passed on within the community by generations of boatmen. At a talk given in the area recently about Recalde, fishermen testified to the accuracy of the sixteenth-century Spanish captain's navigation, identifying by their local names those rocks his chart recorded, and confirming folk memory both of his exploit and the difficulties he faced in achieving it.

Beyond the modern graveyard on the seaward side of the road is Scoil Naomh Gobnait (St Gobnet's School), Dún Chaoin's two-classroom national school, which celebrated its centenary in 2014.

The majority of the children attending the seven remaining schools back west, where they're taught in Irish, go on to attend the co-educational school in Dingle town, which provides post-primary education, also through the medium of Irish. Prior to 2007, when the present school in Dingle opened, post-primary education for the area had been provided in Dingle town since the nineteenth century by the Presentation Nuns, who established a school for girls off Green Street, and the Christian Brothers, whose school for boys was in John Street.

Dunquin from Mount Eagle.

CONVERSATION:
Máire Ní Mhaoileoin

Máire Ní Mhaoileoin is the head teacher of Scoil Naomh Gobnait.

❛I started my own schooling in a national school exactly like this one. Exactly. The same structure, built with two doors so that the girls would go in on the left-hand side and the boys on the right – the more powerful side because the right hand was the hand of God. That way of thinking is gone now. In many ways education here now in Ireland is very different to what it used to be. But from the 1960s they've been trying to close the small schools and amalgamate them. The school I attended was closed and we moved to Ballyferriter, to the building that's now the museum there. That was a building with the boys' door and the girls' door, though we all went in through the one door by then, as far as I remember.

The government is always wanting to close small, rural schools and we're always having to be vigilant because there's huge value in them – not just for the children, but for the area. The local school preserves a certain mentality and a certain way of life. There's something very comforting for people as a community to know that, say, your grandmother or your grandfather were educated in the same rooms before you. It's continuity.

Education was very academic at one stage, when it was payment by results for the teachers – you got paid on the

Plaques on the wall of St Gobnet's school in Dunquin. The motto translates as 'Learning is no burden'.

performance of the children and that went on right into the 1920s. So when the inspector came around the children that couldn't keep up academically would be left at home. That was a bad system. But, at the same time, in the past, there were technical schools you could go on to if you weren't interested in academia – if you wanted to be a builder, say, or a plumber – and your work was just as well respected. Education was very important here, and parents always wanted their children to get on, but there was an underlying ethos that respected work in itself. If you swept the street, what was important to you was that you swept it better than anyone else.

There are always children – whatever the education system has to offer – who'll feel that school isn't for them. And what you say to them is, "we'll just have to plough through it and make life as pleasurable as possible." In small schools you can do that. I remember one day saying to one child who was being difficult, "you know, if you were doing that now all the time, what would happen to the rest of us? Wouldn't we be sad if we didn't get on with each other?" And he thought about it and he said, "We would. You'd be cranky and we'd be cranky. We'd all be cranky together."

You get to know the children and the children get to know you. They have eight years of primary schooling when the classes would be this kind of size. In small communities you have to be very respectful of each other because, if you're not, you're making life very difficult for yourself and for everyone else around you. It's a skill. And the children here have wonderful social skills because of it.

But things are different from how it was long ago, because they socialise more widely now as well. They have the GAA [Gaelic Athletic Association], and they have dancing and gymnastic classes and they'd go in for competitions when they'd meet children from other schools. And they have summer camps. So they meet people from other areas, the way they used not to.

So it's different, but certain things haven't changed. Music has always been a tradition around here. Back in the day, everyone had hundreds of songs leaving national school. They learned them at home, too, but there was always music in the

ABOVE: Traditional music is central to primary education in the Gaeltacht.

RIGHT: A wallchart in Scoil Naomh Gobnait.

classroom. And poetry. Because you have an oral culture here and people were used to learning things by heart – to hearing them, learning them and repeating them: maybe they wouldn't understand what they heard to begin with, but when they grew up they'd understand it. And they'd have it then. It was part of their culture. That hasn't changed. Music and a great respect for words, and for ideas and how to communicate them.

The Irish language, as a language, is a very rich one. An Irish-speaking person here in the past had a huge vocabulary in comparison to the average English speaker anywhere. And these days the vast majority of children here are fluent in two languages, at least. Not only that, but they're aware of language at a very young age, and that has a wonderful effect on learning. In the past, I suppose, some parents here were worried that speaking both Irish and English halved a child's ability to get on in the world. They wanted nothing but English because they felt they were preparing their child for the emigrant boat. But, in fact, studies show that being able to think and speak in different languages doubles and trebles your ability. I see that here now. We'd have a child with a mother who speaks French, say, or whose parents are from abroad, and they'll integrate very easily because the children here would be used to the idea that people have different languages. And that way of thinking stands to children from the area if they go abroad themselves. We'd always assume that, wherever you go, you'd need to learn the language.

We'd want to get inside the mindset of the people in the place we'd go to, because we're reared with a reservoir of proverbs and stories that contains the essence of our own culture.

People know about the Blasket Islanders because of the books that were written there and the outsiders that came in and studied life on the island. They'd know less about the other scholars and poets and writers that came out of the mainland schools. What the islanders had wasn't unusual, but they were unique because they were cut off from the rest of the world, and that gave a sense of difference. There was a wealth of songs and storytelling all round the area, but the island represents a particular moment in time when outsiders became aware of what was here, and recognised it as valuable: and at the same time the island community became super-aware of itself, because it could see it was dying.

Back in the early days when people were coming here to learn the language they'd stay in people's houses and they'd go out and work in the fields alongside the farmers who kept them. It was real integration and that's how they learned. People here learned the same way – by doing things. And they'd always think of a way around a problem. The children will do that from a very young age. They're learning to read in one language and that skill is transferred when they start to read in the second language, so they're used to the concept of skills being transferrable. And if they can't do a thing themselves they'll find someone who can – and that's a skill too. Like, my father wouldn't have been the best farmer in the world but he would know how to fix a milking machine. So if there were problems with milking machines they all came to him to fix them. And old people used to come to him with papers. He was a teacher, and anyone who was teaching at the time – not so much women, but men – people would come to them looking for help with filling out forms and that kind of thing.

That's how it's always worked here, and it's how people still go about things. I saw it myself when I was young. In my own village they got their own water system – their own reservoir, got their own pipes, got it into the houses. What people say here is "nobody's going to do it for you. Do it yourself, work it out."

Dunqin houses beneath Mount Eagle.

'These days when the kids are looking for information they can Google something, but they still have to make it their own. Because if you're working through Irish you have to think about it, and pick and choose, and decide what information you're going to use – you can't just cut and paste. And, you know, it's very easy to explain to children here that it can be dangerous to take things on the Internet at face value. They're used to the idea of getting a second opinion.

We're always vigilant on each other's behalf. Even if you wouldn't have a child in the school yourself you'd value it. We let our politicians know that. If government got a chance they'd close more rural schools, we know they would because it's something that comes around time and again. It's like the post offices. The small schools are the same. You have to protect them.

Homework.

Life here is as rich as it ever was. Richer, maybe. The past has been romanticised. Life was very hard and people were poor and for a long time this place was treated like a reservation. These days you'd be afraid they'd want to turn it into a theme park, and that's not right either. What's here is alive – it is what it is, and it doesn't need to be revived or branded. It needs to be allowed to grow and thrive, and the children are its future.'

In the early 1970s Scoil Naomh Gobnait was one of the schools closed down by the government on the grounds that larger, centralised units were superior and more cost-efficient. The sudden closure without consultation sparked a vociferous local campaign that gained national attention and culminated in a march from Corca Dhuibhne to Dublin. As well as natives of the area, the protestors included regular visitors to Dún Chaoin, and well-wishers from other parts of the country. During the demonstration, which culminated in a sit-in, numbers of campaigners were arrested amid allegations of heavy-handed policing.

The issue was widely debated but the government refused to budge. So, faced with the failure to reverse the official decision, local people ran the school themselves unofficially for three years. Classes were initially held by Breandán and Máire Feiritéar, who taught for a year as volunteers, and subsequently by a young teacher called Mícheál Ó Dubhshláine who had offered himself for the position having witnessed the protest in Dublin. His salary was funded by the community and its supporters.

In 1973, after a change of government, the school was reopened officially. Then Minister for Education Dick Burke, who would later become a European Commissioner, denied absolutely that the reversal of the government's original decision had anything to do with 'any protest or complaints', saying 'the school was reopened for cultural reasons only.'

Mícheál Ó Dubhshláine continued to teach in the school for the next thirty years and, in 1994, gained an honours MA in local history from NUI Maynooth. In the course of his career he published several books about the area, including *A Dark Day on The Blaskets* (Brandon, 2005) and *Inisvickillane* (Brandon, 2009), scholarly and accessible explorations of life

Old schoolbook by cultural revivali Norma Borthwick, illustrated by Jack B. Yeats, first published 1902.

In the past, when the Great Blasket was cut off from the mainland by bad weather, messages were exchanged with the Dún Chaoin community by bonfires on the cliffs.

on the island, both of which were originally issued in Irish. Ó Dubhshláine's educational methods, which were well ahead of their time, included arranging for his pupils to attend schools in Italy and Denmark with the assistance of a European programme for primary schools designed to help in understanding cultural differences. He also had a great interest in theatre, assisting Vlad Znorko, a French dramatist of Polish origin, in establishing a temporary theatre in the area, and encouraging his own pupils to act in local drama productions and travel to France where they performed in theatres in Forbach, Limoges, Lyons and Marseilles. A man 'of vision, philosophy and imagination', he died in 2006 at the age of sixty-four and is buried in Dún Úrlann cemetery, close to the community he served.

HOLY WELLS

The people known as the Corcu Duibhne may have moved westwards from mainland Britain ahead of the expanding Roman Empire, which never extended to Ireland. When Christian missionaries arrived here from Britain some time in the fifth century they applied the common Christian practice of establishing churches and places of worship on sites already sacred to local deities. Over time, spring wells dedicated to their goddess became associated instead with Christian saints.

Many feast or 'pattern' days are still observed in Corca Dhuibhne, though countless others have fallen into disuse. The word 'pattern' is a corruption of 'patron' and refers to the saint to which a well or other holy site is dedicated. Patterns almost always include some sort of circular walk around the site in the direction in which the sun travels.

The feast day of St Gobnet, to whom the little parish church in Dún Chaoin is dedicated, is 11 February and an annual ritual still takes place on that date at the well that bears her name. Sited on a cliff above the ocean, the spring well, which bubbles up between stones, is now marked by a modern bust of the saint carved by the Irish sculptress Cliodhna Cussen.

Patterns involve specific rituals, the details of which are preserved in communal memory. People circle the site, usually three, five, seven, nine or nineteen times, praying. At wells they drink three, or seven, or nine times from their cupped hands. Then the circling may begin again, each round marked by touching a stone or throwing a pebble in the water. Before leaving, something is always left behind, a flower, a feather, a pin, a rag or a coin, emblematic of sacrifice.

In many early societies, seasonal gatherings held at sacred sites appear to have been deemed necessary to promote the balance of the universe: the same belief can be found among indigenous peoples today, such as Native Americans and the Kogi of Colombia. In the past, people came to St Gobnet's pattern from surrounding parishes and from the Blaskets; fairs used always to be held on pattern days, actively incorporating cattle trading, matchmaking and entertainment into the religious observance.

St Gobnet's well on the clifftop at Dunquin.

But the clergy, concerned by the persistence of pagan elements at patterns, systematically attempted to remove what they dismissed as incitement to drunkenness and licentiousness. In the nineteenth and twentieth centuries many patterns were banned on the grounds that they attracted large gatherings and included music and dancing – precisely the elements that the pagan Celts would have seen as creative celebrations of life itself, as personified by the goddess. According to a local story (certainly apocryphal) one priest opposed St Gobnet's pattern so strongly that he cursed the people of Dún Chaoin, who responded by throwing him over the cliff.

Domhnall Mac Síthigh, a local author and folklorist, says that many elements of Early Christianity which themselves retained elements of native pre-Christian ritual and belief survived in the folk tradition until the famine years of the nineteenth century, when communities were fragmented. 'That was the time the big churches were built and the small villages were scattered. The priests told the people that the famine and disease came from God, and they were cowed by fear.'

Now the music and other cultural events that take place on saints' feast days are often held in church halls and community centres and, though the rituals at holy wells retain pagan elements, this separation of celebration from invocation has tended to obscure their origins.

Sure-footed sheep kept in fields bordering Dún Chaoin's precipitous cliffs often scramble down to graze among the rocks above the ocean.

6 The Blasket Centre

The distinctive spine of the Great Blasket island, viewed from Clogher Head.

AS YOU CONTINUE along the Slea Head Drive through Dún Chaoin, a turn to the right would take you up to An Clasach, the high pass that leads between Cruach Mhárthain and Sliabh an Iolair over to Ventry. The etymology of the name Cruach Mhárthain is not certain, though the twentieth-century scholar Pádraig Ó Siochfhradha, a native of Corca Dhuibhne who wrote under the pseudonym '*An Seabhac*' (The Hawk), suggests that it may come from the given name 'Martan': the word '*cruach*' here means 'stack'. According to some versions of the story of the Battle of Ventry, Cruach Mhárthain was the mountain on which Conn Crithir was standing sentry when the forces of the King of the World landed on Ventry Strand.

Beyond the turn for Krugers famous pub you will see signs for the Blasket Centre, Ionad an Bhlascaoid Mhóir, a heritage and cultural centre/museum, honouring the unique community that lived on the Blasket Islands until their evacuation in the 1950s. The centre, which opened in 1993 and is now run by the Office of Public Works (OPW), has a bookshop as well as museum and archive facilities, workshops and language rooms. A restaurant with panoramic views of the islands offers light refreshments, meals and free Wi-Fi. The building has full wheelchair access, designated car parking and special needs toilet facilities, and is available for functions such as wedding ceremonies and conferences. It also

The Blasket Islands from Sliabh an Iolair.

provides a venue for local community events. Opening hours and information can be found on its website: http://blasket.ie/en/

No one knows the origin of the word Blasket. It appears to have been in use by Spanish sailors to identify the island group as early as the sixteenth century and may have been in use much earlier. In the past the group was also known as Ferriter's Islands, after the Anglo-Norman Ferriter family to whom it was leased by the Fitzgerald Earls of Desmond from the thirteenth century. When the Fitzgeralds were dispossessed under the reign of Elizabeth I at the end of the sixteenth century, the islands were granted to Sir Richard Boyle who continued to lease them to the Ferriters. Stones from a Ferriter castle on the Great Blasket were used in 1840 to build a Protestant school there. This school was closed down about ten years later, after the Great Famine, and island children were subsequently educated in a national school, established in 1864. The last Ferriter to control the islands was the chieftain and poet Piaras Feirtéar, who was hanged by the English Commonwealth authorities during the Cromwellian conquest of Ireland (1649–53). Today local people generally refer to the Great Blasket as 'the island' and you may notice that they speak of going 'into' rather than 'onto' it. In comparatively recent times Inis Tuaisceart ('north island') has been referred to as 'The Sleeping Giant'. Local people generally call it *An Fear Marbh* ('the dead man'). Both names arise from its appearance when seen from a distance.

Inis Tuaisceart, the most northerly of the Blasket Islands, was inhabited in Early Christian times and, for short periods, in the nineteenth century.

There is evidence of Early Christian monastic settlement on the Great Blasket and, since there is a source of spring water on three of the islands, it is likely that the group was occupied fairly continuously from earliest times. It may be, however, that there were periods when the islands were deserted and certainly the number of inhabitants would have fluctuated: we know, for example, that when families evicted by Lord Ventry relocated there in the late nineteenth century they augmented an already existing community primarily located in the now-ruined village that can still be seen from the mainland.

Before turning to sea fishing with the introduction of seine boats and *naomhóga*, the nineteenth-century islanders engaged primarily in agriculture. They also fished with lines from the cliffs and hunted seabirds, rabbits and seals for meat. Although they considered roasted crabs a delicacy, they seldom ate lobsters and were surprised to discover that outsiders were willing to pay for them. In 1907 the islands were purchased by the Congested Districts Board, which built several new houses and made other improvements on the Great Blasket, including a new slipway. Between the setting up of the independent state and the evacuation of the last inhabitants of the island – a period of economic depression throughout the country – few, if any, farther improvements were made. In 2009 the OPW bought most of the property on the Great Blasket, including the deserted village, and the state is now the majority landowner. Guided tours were launched in 2010 and plans are under way for the preservation and conservation of the old village.

Up to the end of the nineteenth century the islanders were accustomed to bailiffs and land agents demanding rent arrears and seizing fishing-gear and boats in lieu of payment. As a result they were suspicious of visitors. That attitude changed at the turn of the twentieth century with the arrival of scholars who were willing to pay for accommodation and showed interest in the language and customs of the islands. The Irish playwright J. M. Synge, who visited briefly in 1905 on the advice of W. B. Yeats, wrote about his experiences in a collection of essays illustrated by the poet's brother Jack B. Yeats (*In Wicklow, West Kerry and Connemara.* Maunsel, 1911). Synge stayed in the house of the island 'king', one of whose daughters is believed to have been the inspiration for

Pegeen Mike, the heroine of his best known work, *The Playboy of The Western World*.

In 1907, the Norwegian linguist and scholar of Old Irish, Carl Marstrander, known to the islanders as 'The Viking', came to the Great Blasket to learn Irish. He stayed with Tomás Ó Criomhthain, who became his teacher and friend. The eventual result of this visit and their relationship was *An tOileánach* (The Islandman), a classic autobiography from Ó Criomhthain, which was followed by a flow of other works written or dictated by the last generation to live on the island, and their descendants.

Tomás Ó Criomhthain.

In 1910 Marstrander taught Old Irish in the School of Irish Learning in Dublin, where one of his students was the English scholar and poet Robin Flower. On the Norwegian's advice Flower visited the Great Blasket, stayed at the house of the 'king' and became a friend and pupil of Ó Criomhthain. Flower, who was in his late twenties when he first visited the island, returned repeatedly until his death in 1946 and was loved and admired by its people. Along with two other Englishmen, the Classicist George Thomson and the Celtic scholar Kenneth Jackson – and building on relationships originally established by Marstrander – he encouraged the islanders to dictate and write books in their own language about their lives and the people around them.

These works, known collectively as the Blasket Literature, are fascinating, not least because their authors were aware of the irony and complexity of a situation in which what they perceived as their duty to their oral culture demanded that they turn to writing. Produced within a few decades by a dying community, the core books in the canon are both revealing and frustrating in terms of what their authors and editors chose to include and leave out.

The village on the Great Blasket before the 1953 evacuation.
COURTESY OPW BLASKET CENTRE

Throughout the early twentieth century Irish students and scholars, many of whom were inspired by Ireland's cultural revivalist movement, were part of the process of facilitating the books' publication. Among them was Brian Ó Ceallaigh who arrived on the island in 1917 with a letter of introduction to Tomás Ó Criomhthain from Pádraig Ó Siochfhradha. Ó Ceallaigh read works by Pierre Loti and Maxim Gorky to Ó Criomhthain and encouraged him to believe that his own work, originally written as a diary, ought to be published. With Ó Ceallaigh's editorial assistance, extracts from the diary were published in 1928 as *Allagar na hInise,* edited by Ó Siochfhradha and published by Ó Fallmhain Teo; *Island Cross-Talk*, a translation by Tim Enright, was published in 1986 by the Oxford University Press. Ó Criomhthain's autobiography *An tOileánach* followed *Allagar na hInise* in 1929, with the same editor and publisher. Translations into five languages have since been made of

Peig Sayers with two visitors to the island, (l) Niamh (Martha) Nic Gearailt and (r) Helen Killenan. COURTESY OPW BLASKET CENTRE

it from *The Islandman,* a beautiful English translation by Robin Flower published by the Talbot Press, Dublin, in 1943 and the Oxford University Press, in 1951. An unabridged version of Ó Criomhthain's full text was published by the Talbot Press in 2002.

Undoubtedly the most notorious of the islanders' books was and remains *Peig*: the reflections of Peig (Peg) Sayers, an elderly woman, famed as a storyteller, who dictated her book to her son. Originally edited by Máire Ní Chinnéide, a cultural nationalist who was active in the War of Independence, the book has remained in print since its publication in 1936 by the Talbot Press, and has been translated into French, German and English.

Certainly, there were readers who enjoyed and appreciated *Peig* but it became anathema to many Irish people who – not understanding the context in which it was written, and resenting the educational policy that made it compulsory reading for schoolchildren

– associated it with irrelevance and coercion, accusations that have bedevilled the Irish language since the founding of the state. Since the late 1990s, with the lifting of the requirement to achieve a pass grade in Irish in order to pass the secondary schools' Leaving Certificate examination, *Peig* has steadily been rehabilitated in the national consciousness; and while it remains on the school syllabus it is no longer required reading.

The iconic status of the Blasket Literature owed much to the newly established Irish state's increasing tendency to equate simplicity and perceived cultural purity with a sense of national identity that was closely linked to its relationship with the Roman Catholic Church. Perhaps because it begins and ends with devout reflections on death, many Irish schoolchildren thought of *Peig* and its author as 'miserable'. But, while it has none of the erotic comedy, grotesque exaggeration and irreverent irony that belongs to the native Irish tradition of storytelling – and in which Peig, according to local people, delighted – it offers a window on a world in which neither rural poverty nor a sense of spirituality imply a lack of sophistication. There is no doubt, however, that it describes a life that had little in common with the experience of most mid-twentieth-century Irish teenagers.

An interesting footnote to the island's history of welcoming outsiders links it to the extensive reach of the Nazi German propaganda machine. Ludwig Muhlhausen, a leading German linguist and Celtologist, spent time on the Great Blasket and in other Gaeltacht areas in the 1920s and was given the Chair of Celtic Studies in Berlin in 1935, when its previous incumbent Julius Pokorny was removed because of his Jewish ancestry. In 1939, at the behest of Goebbels's Ministry of Propaganda, Muhlhausen inaugurated a series of radio talks in the Irish language, broadcast in order to bolster Ireland's neutrality in the war and to whip up Irish antagonism against the Allies. After the war ended it was established that he had used his time in the Gaeltacht to take hundreds of photographs of the western seaboard which informed preparations for an aborted Nazi invasion of Ireland, codenamed Operation Green.

The islands had no church or consecrated graveyard. Unbaptised infants were buried on the Great Blasket at a site above the White Strand, the beach that can be seen from the mainland. Otherwise

ABOVE: Explorations of the Blasket Literature and way of life continue to be published.

LEFT: The cliff path to Dún Chaoin Pier today.

the dead were brought in their coffins to the mainland and carried up the steep cliff path in Dún Chaoin for burial there. Tomás Ó Criomhthain, who was born on the Great Blasket in 1856, died in his home in 1937 and is buried in the graveyard by the parish church of Naomh Gobnait in Dún Chaoin. Careful restoration of his house on the island is being undertaken with funds from central government. In 1942, after the death of her husband and the emigration of her children to America, Peig Sayers left the island and returned to Dún Chaoin, where she was born in 1873 in the small village of Baile an Bhiocáire (Vickarstown). She died in Dingle hospital in 1958 and is buried in Dún Chaoin burial ground, facing the island where she spent her married life. The official date for the evacuation of the last Blasket inhabitants was 1953, though some families held on for at least another year and/or continued to return in summertime. Sheep continue to be grazed on Beag Inis (The Little Island), the smallest of the group, which was used by the islanders for the same purpose.

Dáithí de Mórdha

Dáithí de Mórdha of the OPW Blasket Centre, was born and raised in Dún Chaoin, where he now lives with his wife and children.

❝ I grew up with the islanders all around me. My grandparents lived in the house with us and my grandfather used to fish with islanders, so when I first knew them they were just people who would be in my house, fishermen and farmers who lived around me here on the mainland and were my neighbours. And then, I suppose, when you grow up and you start reading their books maybe, you realise that there's something special about the island that sets it apart. But the Blaskets and Dún Chaoin were always part of the same parish. Their folktales are the same as our folktales, their songs – apart from one or two – are the same as ours. So is their music, at least you'd think so. But, maybe because I study them now so closely, I can see that the way they speak is a bit different from the way we speak, and their music is a bit wilder. But it's still a fact that their culture and the mainland culture were one.

An tOileánach was published in 1929 and after that you had the boom of the Blasket Literature. And I suppose individuals like Tomás and Peig were held up as giants or icons of "Gaelic Ireland". Then a myth got created in which the island was a kind of Utopia where nobody ever fell out with each other, nobody ever died of hunger and no woman was ever worn out by constant pregnancy or had to face complications in childbirth without a doctor. Everything about it was supposed to be perfect. We'd still have people getting in touch with us here now, researchers who'd say "tell me about this pure version of the Irish language". Well, the Blasket Irish wasn't any purer than the Irish spoken on the mainland at the time. Compared to the Irish that we speak now there's a huge difference because we have 24-hour television and radio and Internet and everything so our Irish is more influenced by English. But that's another thing again. The idea that the islanders had some kind of pure version of Irish in their time is as daft as the notion that Peig Sayers was praying from morning to night. That was just the new state trying to create some kind of ideology or identity for itself. The Peig Sayers that the people here knew is not the person in the book.

I did my own Leaving Cert in 2000 – which I think was the first year that *Peig* wasn't compulsory – and the teachers were still battling with forty, fifty years of resistance to it. When I first started working here I remember Irish people would come in and you'd see the life drain from their faces when they'd see a photo of Peig. And it's a thing that's still felt. But, then, compulsion always has a negative effect. I remember having to study Jane Austen's *Emma* and I hated it. I mean, that was a book that made no sense at all to a bunch of lads in the Christian Brothers' school in Dingle at the end of the 1990s. I remember looking at questions on an exam paper and I couldn't handle it. So I just

Cover of an Irish satirical magazine from 1936 showing a publisher exporting a boatload of manuscripts from the Great Blasket.
COURTESY OPW BLASKET CENTRE

Early twentieth century photograph of boys on the Great Blasket island with donkeys used as pack animals. COURTESY OPW BLASKET CENTRE

wrote, "I refuse to answer these questions because I feel they are culturally biased against me." I thought that was very smart! But the fact is that the compulsion ruined that whole period of literature for me. Even now I hate it. I can't even enjoy the costume dramas on television.

In the nineteenth century and early twentieth century, as a pre-Capitalist, almost Communist, community where money didn't exchange hands and monetary wealth wasn't important, wealth was having four cows or two bulls or whatever. But once people started selling lobsters and getting money into their hands, and emigrants were sending home letters saying "we bought a house" or "we bought a new car", the wealth went from being something associated with the land and the sea to something you put in your pocket. That changed the whole

Schoolchildren outside the Great Blasket's national school *c.* 1935.
COURTESY OPW BLASKET CENTRE

dynamic, and it accelerated the abandonment of the island because you couldn't show your wealth in there, and you couldn't earn money in there.

I think perhaps that when emigrants from the island went to America and found that the island books were known and valued internationally they became even more proud of their roots here. Because there was certainly discrimination here in Ireland against the islanders at one time, and not just in Dingle where they might have been seen as wild or a bit uncouth. There were times when they were treated as outsiders in rural communities here on the mainland – there are stories of them being treated that way at weddings and gatherings sometimes. So, in a way, who they were and where they came from was validated in America and elsewhere by the island books.

In the country as a whole, when the new state was set up, the creation of a kind of Irish-speaking, hurling, dancing-at-the-crossroads, leprechaun-ridden myth arose from the need to assert and establish a separate identity from England. It was very understandable. And, in a way, the island books fed into the myth, which was bound up with the Catholic religion. But the truth, of course, was far more complicated. Peig, who was set up as a kind of Holy Catholic Mother Ireland figure, was actually descended from English Protestants. Tomás, who wrote in Irish, says that his cousins on the mainland taught him to write.

But he never mentions the fact that, up to when he was about ten years old, there was a Protestant school on the island which taught the kids Irish and that, at the time, the national schools didn't teach them to write Irish at all. So it's much more likely that he learned to write at – or at least as a result of the presence of – the Protestant school on the island. But he ignores the fact that it was even there. And why is that? Because it doesn't fit the narrative of 1930s Ireland.

The scholars from the outside, the editors, the fact that a lot of the island books were published by state publishing houses, they all came together to create the Blasket Literature and the myth that comes with it. What's important is that we don't lose sight of what the literature itself is – which is a collection of some of the most important folk literature this country has.

Heritage to me is a living thing. You have to be researching it, you have to be asking questions about it – which is what the research library here is for. We've always been very happy for people who want to use it to call and make an appointment so we can show them around and they can see what's here.

And my own philosophy is that you can't have a building like this which deals with heritage without opening it up to the community, not just for us to display our heritage but to develop it. So we do things like concerts and seminars and conferences about different aspects of life here. Local development groups have meetings here. The schools do plays. At the height of the summer there are twenty people employed here. They're not all full-time but they make a difference to the community. My own little girls go to the school in Dún Chaoin, which is where I went and their grandfather went. My wife grew up in London – her parents had emigrated from here, which was the case with a lot of people in the area. I'd like to think that there'd be employment and housing for our kids at home if they want to stay and settle down here.

THE ISLAND KING

The title of 'king' of the Blasket Islands was not hereditary: it simply indicated his acknowledged role as a leader qualified to arbitrate in disputes, coordinate the rundale system and mediate with outside authorities. The last king, or Rí, was Pádraig Ó Catháin, the island postman, who held the position for twenty-five years until his death in 1929. He was a commanding figure who could speak and read English and, because he made regular trips to the mainland to collect and deliver post, it was he who welcomed visitors and was a point of contact with them between visits. Scholars and others who visited the islands made the trip to and from the Great Blasket in his *naomhóg* and were often accommodated in his house.

Effectively, the Rí was first among equals, a man who emerged from the community by no established system of election. On the Blaskets there were periods between the tenures of individual kings when the title slipped into abeyance, either because no one was deemed suitable to hold it or because

Visitors to the Great Blasket were accommodated in family dwellings where they shared the communal way of life.
COURTESY OPW BLASKET CENTRE

conditions at the time provoked no need to seek a candidate. The only Irish community that continues to maintain the role of Rí is in Tory Island in the Donegal Gaeltacht. But the function and title represent the survival of a form of social organisation once common throughout Ireland, which echoes similar systems in historic and prehistoric societies worldwide.

Among the foreign scholars who spent time on the Great Blasket in the early twentieth century was George Thomson, an English academic who came there to study Irish. A Classicist and a student of Marxian philosophy, he first visited in 1923, when he lodged with Pádraig Ó Catháin's daughter. Thomson perceived surviving social and cultural resonances in the island community that linked it with historical society prior to the development of private property as a means of production. He was also fascinated by the echoes of Classical Greek storytelling in the islanders' oral tradition, and his Irish-language translations of Greek texts were greatly admired by them. In 1933 he personally financed the publication of the islander Muiris Ó Súilleabháin's *Fiche Blian ag Fás* (Twenty Years Growing), having previously facilitated an English-language version, *Twenty Years A-Growing*, with a foreword by the novelist E. M. Forster. In 1976 he brought the Irish version back into print, in collaboration with Monsignor Pádraig Ó Fiannachta. Thomson was also a Shakespearian scholar and translated a number of the bard's sonnets into Irish.

During the 1930s, convinced that the Irish government of the time supported the language with a view to stagnating, if not reversing, social progress, Thomson conceived an initiative to offer Gaeltacht communities a modern education in the Irish language 'so that they could adapt their culture to modern conditions'. To his lifelong regret, his vision was rejected by the Irish Department of Education and, after a brief period as a lecturer in Greek through Irish at University College Galway, he returned to a distinguished academic career in England. He continued to contribute to Irish-Hellenic Studies until his death in 1987.

An Tiaracht, the most westerly island of the Blasket group.

Part of the island's iconic status derives from a melancholy statement made by an ageing man who was fully aware that he lived at the end of an era. Among the slogans on souvenir T-shirts in Dingle are the words '*Ní Bheidh Mo Leithéid Arís Ann*', which translates as 'My Like (one such as I am) will not exist again.' It's a version of one of the most quoted lines from *An tOileánach*, '*Ní bheidh ár leithéidí arís ann*', 'The likes of us (people such as we are) will not exist again'.

That statement by Ó Criomhain contains an imaginatively related association with one of the oldest images in Celtic mythology, and one of Ireland's most popular legends. Hy-Brasil, an island cloaked in mist, was said by the Celts to exist somewhere in the western Atlantic, visible once every seven years but impossible to reach. Scholars have associated it with The Isles of the Blessed, or Fortunate Isles, inhabited by the heroes of Greek mythology. One of the best-known stories about Fionn and the Fianna concerns Fionn's son Oisín who meets a beautiful woman riding a white horse

The awe-inspiring effects of light at the end of the Dingle Peninsula have contributed to its ancient heritage of myth and folklore.

by the Atlantic Ocean and, smitten by love, travels with her to Tír na nÓg (The Land of Youth).

Tír na nÓg is a land flowing with milk and honey, where trees bloom all year round and heroes hunt and feast. But after three years there Oisín longs to return to visit his companions and, eventually, the woman lends him her horse with the warning that if he touches the ground in Ireland he will never see her again. Having ridden across the waves, he finds three men on the Atlantic shoreline trying to lift a rock. Astonished by their weakness, he leans from his saddle to help them but the girth breaks and he falls. As soon as he touches the ground, the horse rises in the air and flies westwards across the ocean and, seeing Oisín lying on the beach, the men are terrified. No longer a tall, powerful hero, he has become an ancient greybeard, hardly able to stand. The three years he thought he had spent in The Land of Youth were in fact 300, and the life he knew and the people he loved were long since dead and gone.

The phrase '*Oisín i ndíaidh na Féinne*', which means 'Oisín (left behind) after the Fianna' is still used in spoken Irish to describe someone bereft of the people, way of life or worldview with whom or with which s/he grew up.

7 From Clogher to The Three Sisters

The cliffs at Clogher.

BEYOND DÚN CHAOIN the Slea Head Drive begins to turn eastwards, curving around the bulk of Cruach Mhárthain. The views continue to be stunning and there are places to pull in by the roadside if you wish to stop. At An Cloichear ('the stony place'), there is a small beach enclosed by dramatic cliffs, a fine place to take photographs but dangerous for bathing: it is important to obey the signs here and elsewhere that warn of dangerous currents. On the main road, before you reach the beach, is Louis Mulcahy's Pottery Workshop. It has a shop, a café serving home-made food, and a small bookshop, and often you can see a professional thrower going through the daily routine of throwing pots. Mulcahy and his Danish wife, the weaver Lisbeth Mulcahy, came to the area from Dublin in the 1970s with the aim of developing a studio/workshop that would leave an indelible print on the long-term history of Irish handcraft. On arrival they embraced the Irish language and raised their family to speak it. Now an internationally recognised potter and one of the largest employers

Clogher Strand with Louis Mulcahy's Pottery Workshop in the distance.

ABOVE LEFT: Sheep farming is one of the principal agricultural practices in the area.
ABOVE RIGHT: A Louis Mulcahy pot outside his workshop in Cloichear.

west of Dingle, Mulcahy became the first Irish craftsman to receive an honorary degree from the National University of Ireland in recognition both of his artistry and of the prosperity it has brought to his community. All Mulcahy pottery is produced in the workshop in Cloichear where he continues to provide creative input and his son now runs the business.

Beyond Cloichear a left-hand turn as you approach Ballyferriter village will take you into the farmland between the main road and the rugged coastline that stretches round to Ceann Sibéal (Sybil Head) and the distinctive three peaks known in English as The Three Sisters. Ceann Sibéal Golf Course offers the most westerly links in Europe; the club was founded in 1924 and Ireland's Ryder Cup hero Christy O'Connor Jr. oversaw an update to the course and clubhouse in the 1990s.

This is a good area for bicycling and for long, rambling walks on the roads and along the cliffs, away from the main routes. If you plan to cross a field, look and see if there's a local person you can ask before you do so, and read and obey signs and notices about privacy. Be aware that land can be boggy and that gates must be left as you find them. Dogs must be kept on leads on private land and, as a rule of thumb, should not be taken into fields where animals are grazing. Towards the end of the summer you'll see large bales of silage stacked in fields and farmyards, shrink-wrapped in heavy black plastic: this is grass that has been cut and compacted, without first being dried, to use as animal feed in the winter. The sound of silage cutting can

The Three Sisters viewed from above Clogher Strand.

be heard throughout the long evenings here in late summer and the contractors' machines for cutting, and trailers for transporting it, are a familiar sight on the roads.

To the east, below The Three Sisters, is a small headland called Dún an Óir where much of what may have been an Iron Age fortified promontory has fallen into the ocean. The name means 'the fort of gold', which may be a mistranslation for *Dún an Áir* (The Fort of Slaughter). This was the scene of the bloody siege that ended a sixteenth-century attempt by mainland European powers to support the assimilated Norman-Irish overlords of the native Irish in their rebellion against English administration in Ireland. In 1580, following an earlier attempt initiated by James Fitzmaurice Fitzgerald, about 600 Italian and Spanish Papal troops commanded by Sebastiano di San Giuseppe landed at Smerwick (a name which derives from the Norse words '*smoer*' and '*wick*', meaning 'butter harbour'). An attempt to link up with the Munster Irish forces was thwarted by the English under Thomas Butler, 10th Earl of Ormond, and Arthur Grey, 14th Baron Grey de Wilton, and the invaders' ships were blockaded. San Giuseppe retreated to Dún an Óir and attempted to strengthen and defend the existing fortifications there. The garrison, which included men and women, was pinned down between Grey's land forces, based in Dingle, and English naval ships which landed munitions and supplies at Smerwick Harbour.

The remaining promontory at Dún an Óir.

On 10 November 1580, after a three-day siege under artillery fire, San Giuseppe surrendered. There are conflicting accounts as to the terms agreed but the outcome was massacre.

According to a dispatch from Lord Grey to Elizabeth I of England dated 11 November 1580, he required the besieged Spanish and Italians, and the Irish and English Catholics who were with them, to surrender without preconditions, and rejected a request for a ceasefire. He informed the queen that an agreement was made for an unconditional surrender, with hostages taken by his forces to ensure compliance. The morning after the surrender an English force entered the fort to secure and guard armaments and supplies. Grey's account says 'Then put I in certain bands of men, who straight fell to execution. There were six hundred slain', and that he spared those of higher rank: 'those that I gave life unto, I have bestowed upon the captains and gentlemen that hath well deserved ...' The Irishmen and an English Catholic among those who were spared are said to have been offered life if they would renounce their faith. Local tradition has it that, on refusal, their arms and legs were broken in three places by an ironsmith and that after a day and night in agony, they were hanged.

Two other roughly contemporary Irish accounts say that Grey promised the garrison their lives in return for their surrender. A letter describing the siege sent to the Earl of Leicester by the English officer Richard Bingham, who was present, blamed the massacre on sailors acting without orders. However, another English account, written in 1587 by John Hooker, states that Grey's troops were the executioners, and that one of their leaders was Captain (later Sir Walter) Raleigh: three decades later, when Raleigh had fallen from royal favour, his involvement in the massacre was brought against him as a criminal charge in one of his trials, when he argued that he was 'obliged to obey the commands of his superior officer'. At the time of the siege Elizabeth congratulated Grey, then Lord Deputy of Ireland, on being an instrument of God's glory, and criticised him for having spared any of his captives.

This massacre and others in Munster during the same period were part of a deliberate strategy intended to deter both future attempts at rebellion in Ireland and proposed invasion from Europe in its support. It was underpinned by a ruthless scorched-earth policy that devastated the civilian population: Dingle town was sacked and burned twice within three years, with much of its population fleeing west and into the mountains, where the country people also sought safety.

According to local folklore, the execution of the Dún an Óir captives took two days, with many of the bodies thrown into the ocean after being beheaded in a field still known as Gort a Ghearradh, which means 'the field of the cutting'. Another local field, known as Gort na gCeann (The Field of the Heads), was investigated in recent years by archaeologists and found to be full of sixteenth-century skulls.

The massacre at Dún an Óir is commemorated by a modern sculpture by Cliodhna Cussen, which stands on the headland, and nearby boards provide information for visitors.

Cliodhna Cussen's memorial to the victims of the 1580 massacre at Dún an Óir.

CONVERSATION:
Maidhc Ó Mainín

Maidhc Ó Mainín farms land located between Sybil Head and The Three Sisters, which has been in his family for generations, and fishes off the surrounding coast as his father did before him. His wife, Ann Marie Sears, whose people come from the area, grew up in America, where Maidhc worked for about five years from the late 1980s. Their children go to the school at Dún Chaoin.

❝ One of the biggest changes here is the number of people who are left in the villages. When I was growing up if you walked through a village there were always people outside doing things, and kids playing on the roads. You couldn't be on the roads now because of the cars and buses. And back then you'd be in everybody else's house as much as you'd be in your own house. There'd be some house in the village and everyone would be in there every evening. Smaller families and emigration, I suppose, have changed that. The money is a lot better in cities. Then again, in the city people move house and it makes no difference to them, but here you'd have your house on your own land and that's your home. I suppose that's what people come back to.

The names of places and things and how people lived are passed on here. Like, in the past, every village had pattern days, but the Church got rid of that. The way it was back then, if you think about it, say you'd go into a graveyard for a funeral and they'd be digging the grave and old bones might be thrown up. And there'd be a skull and you'd sit down and be talking to it and praying. That was a custom. And that would be your grandfather's skull or some ancestor's, because that's where your family had always been buried.

FROM CLOGHER TO THE THREE SISTERS

My grandfather used to go down the cliffs getting seagulls eggs. People ate them. And when we were young if there were sheep stuck down on the cliffs we'd go down after them. If they went down you had to get them up some way. And you'd fall just as fast as your grandfather would have fallen. And, the same thing, in the past if there was a wreck, a shipwreck, and stuff was thrown in from it, they'd go down to get things. It was dangerous, I suppose, but they'd get them. One time there was a cargo ship loaded with timber and there was a very bad storm and the cargo was let go – it was put overboard. I don't know, I was young, it was in the early 1980s or something, and there were old fellows there in their seventies – men that could never swim – and they were out in the water getting planks of timber, and they gathered it in the water and pushed it in to the women. You were supposed to give it back if things came in to you. But when the guards came round looking, they never found it. Nobody had any timber!

My grandfather would have spoken a bit of French. There was a Frenchman, Pierre Trehiou, used to come around and buy lobsters. He had a big storage ship and he'd come round and go right up the coast. He came here and he went into the island, and the fishermen picked up enough French to speak to him. And, I suppose, he learned a bit of Irish. The men would be used to foreign sailors and they'd talk to them. Trehiou would give the islanders tobacco and things on credit and when he'd come back again he'd knock the price off what he'd give them for the lobsters.

Modern lobster pots, as used around the Dingle Peninsula.

When I went to America there wasn't much work around here. I went away fishing first and then I was on the sites in America, building. There was always some kind of a half tradesman around here that'd you'd work with when you were growing up, and you'd learn from him. People had different trades. When I was young, the forge at Burnham was a busy place, say. Very busy. But people go away, or when a man dies there's no son to take over.

My neighbour, he was the first man to get a tractor here. In 1952 he got a tractor, before that it was all horses. I don't know, I think he bought the tractor and a trailer and a plough for £300. He got most of that as a loan. And he got the tractor in the spring, and by the next spring he'd bought the machine that cut the hay and cut the corn – and he had paid off his loan by then because he had worked day and night with the tractor and the trailer and the plough, taking it round to every village and ploughing for them. It's like the lads with the big machines that go round cutting the silage now. They're all local lads and it costs a heap of money to get the machines, and you'd have to renew them every few years, and the prices of everything would be going up and down all the time, so you're taking a risk.

Whole villages used to be working together making the hay, and then the farmers moved on from that to the silage. They kept it in pits. I suppose when the people left it turned into a contractor job. Then, I don't know, I think the winters got more severe and the plastic you'd have covering the pits won't stay on

Cattle in a farmyard near Ballyferriter.

Rough seas near Clogher Head.

in bad winters. It's an awful job altogether to get up in the morning after a bad night and look at plastic up in the air and the whole pit uncovered. Now the machines bale it and you have it there in the yard brought in to you. The gales are worse now and the winds are worse than they used to be.

Two years or three years ago the EU were abolishing quotas on milk here and the farming organisations were telling all the farmers to expand. All the young farmers went to the banks and borrowed money and put up big new buildings and bought cows and high-bred animals – I don't know are they animals or not really, they wouldn't live here in the winter anyway if they had to be outside. And then the price of milk dropped and the man that stayed with his twenty or thirty cows there all the time is doing way better than the man who's trying to pay back what he borrowed from the bank.

It's different on the mixed farms. Sheep might be good one year, cattle might be good the next year – and it might be the fishing that was good the year after that. If you were stuck doing just the one thing the whole time, you'd get bored, maybe. And, the thing is, it's better for the land, which is more important than yourself, really, because you'll be gone in the end. I don't know if

I'd be optimistic or not about what will happen in the future. It doesn't really matter as long as you carry on what's been there before you, and pass it on, and leave the place the way it was, or a small bit better.

Some of the place names here are ancient. If you look at The Three Sisters, the farthest peak is called Binn Diarmada, [Diarmad's Peak]. That's from a story about Fionn and the Fianna. Diarmad was a companion of Fionn's who came from Corca Dhuibhne – his name was Diarmad Ua Duibhne because this was his territory. Binn Méanach, the name people call the second one, means "the middle peak". Then you get the name of the third one written down as Binn Hánraí [Henry's Peak] and nowadays it's pronounced "Been Aown ree". But in folklore it's called Binn Shean-Draoi, which means "The Old Druid's Peak", and that's pronounced "Been Haown Dree". You can see how English settlers and mapmakers would have problems writing that name down and trying to translate it. You get approximations of old names on maps all the time. They'd hear it as "Henry's Peak" because Henry is *Anroí* in Irish. But "The Old Druid's Peak" links the first and the third peak to the stories of the Fianna, and that makes sense of both names.

Here every ditch has a name, and every field has a name, and every cove has a name, and every rock has a name out at sea. The names are something you're supposed to mind, and I suppose you do if you're a farmer or a fisherman. If you don't, they're gone. 〞

Teasels growing on the cliff above Smerwick Harbour, looking towards The Three Sisters.

J. M. Synge, writing at the turn of the twentieth century about the Aran Islands in the Connacht Gaeltacht, observed the custom of keening over skulls unearthed in graveyards that Maidhc describes.

In his book *The Celts: A Chronological History* (The Collins Press 2002), the Irish historian Dáithí Ó hÓgáin quotes from the ancient Roman writer Florus who, commenting on a campaign along the eastern Danube, deplores the Celtic custom of 'offering human blood to the gods' and 'drinking from men's skulls'. According to Ó hÓgáin, this is likely to have been an accidental or deliberate misrepresentation of the ancient Celtic reverence for the head as the centre of power and wisdom within the body: other Roman commentators recognised that skulls of powerful enemies were decorated with gold and used as holy vessels.

The English poet Edmund Spenser, author of *The Faerie Queene,* an epic poem in praise of Queen Elizabeth, is said to have been present at the siege of Dún an Óir, and his work *A Veue of the present state of Irelande* (1596) is partly a defence of Lord Grey, who greatly influenced his thinking on Ireland as an English colony.

Spenser wrote that Ireland was a 'diseased portion' of the English state that 'must first be cured and reformed, before it could be in a position to appreciate the good sound laws and blessings of the nation'. In his view, Ireland's native laws, customs and religion combined to create a disruptive and degraded people, and he advocated the eradication of the Irish language on the grounds that it undermined English authority. 'Soe that the speach being Irish, the hart must needes be Irishe; for out of the aboundance of the hart, the tonge speaketh'.

As a poet himself, Spenser was interested in Ireland's native bardic poetry, and says that he caused several poems to be translated for him. In his opinion, they 'savoured of sweet wit and good invention'. But, noting that the traditional role of the bards was to record and praise the rule of local chieftains, and to satirise those who opposed them, he denounced the composition of bardic poetry as an evil custom in need of 'reformation'.

From a creative point of view, traditional Irish poetry can be said to have stagnated by Spenser's time, becoming increasingly rigid and formal both in composition and performance. It is possible that, had it survived and developed unsuppressed, it might have been reformed by the poets themselves, such as Piaras Féirtéar whose work, while still traditional, shows originality. But *A Veue of the present state of Irelande* advocated Grey's scorched-earth policy as the most effective way of reforming Irish society and bringing it to an appreciation of the good sound laws and blessings of Elizabeth's nation. Spenser, who was a witness, cited its success in Munster:

> Out of everye corner of the woode and glenns they came creepinge forth upon theire handes, for theire legges could not beare them; they looked Anatomies [of] death, they spake like ghostes, crying out of theire graves; they did eate of the carrions, happye wheare they could find them, yea, and one another soone after, in soe much as the verye carcasses they spared not to scrape out of theire graves; and if they found a plott of water-cresses or shamrockes, theyr they flocked as to a feast... in a shorte space there were none almost left, and a most populous and plentyfull countrye suddenly lefte voyde of man or beast ...

These were the farmers and fishermen whose homes, crops and boats had been burned, whose cattle were driven off and whose property was looted in the struggle between Elizabeth's administration and the assimilated Anglo-Norman Fitzgeralds whose native Irish Brehon lawyers and bardic poets upheld their right to rule here and across all of Munster.

Ironically, the only contemporary outsider's description we have of Irish bardic poetry is a line in Spenser's book saying that the poems he had had translated 'soe that I might understande them' were 'sprinckled with some prettye flowers of theire owne naturall

Ruined Fitzgerald stronghold at Rahinnane, above Ventry, destroyed in the fifteenth century.

devise, which gave good grace and comlines [comeliness] unto them'. Over the next two centuries the native legal, administrative and cultural systems continued to be systematically suppressed and widely eradicated.

DINNSEANCHAS

The modern Irish word '*dinnseanchas*' comes from two words in Old Irish, '*dind*' meaning 'place' and '*senchas*' meaning 'old stories', 'ancient history, or 'tradition'. In early Irish literature it refers to specific collections of poems and prose that deal with the origins of place names. Many of these stories, and many others belonging to more recent local place names, are passed on from generation to generation in the living oral tradition of contemporary Gaeltacht areas.

Many place names given in the manuscripts existed long before the stories that purport to explain their origins. Often the explanations were contrived long afterwards to justify the territorial claims of kings and chieftains by linking their ancestry with ancient heroes and gods. For thousands of years they formed an important part of the education of the native Irish elite: a knowledge of the landscape was important for military leaders; and an ability to recite the origins of place names was required of the hereditary bardic poets who were attached to ruling families in Ireland as late as the mid-seventeenth century.

Dinnseanchas is incorporated into saga texts about legendary heroes such as Cú Chulainn and Fionn Mac Cumhaill as well as in the folk tradition. Folktales about the names of landmarks, and even particular fields, are still told today. They can be among the best starting places for a conversation in a local pub or with your host in a rural B&B. And not all *dinnseanchas* is ancient or even aristocratic – the story of why two places at the end of the peninsula are both called Ballydavid offers a window into the area's colonial history, for example. And, while the exact etymology remains uncertain, the reason why local people call Ballyferriter "An Buailtín" gives insights into the vanished farming methods of its small, interdependent communities.

8 Ballyferriter

Ballyferriter village.

MANY OF THE SMALLER VILLAGES such as Peig Sayers' home place, Baile Bhiocáire, do not appear on road signage. Their names, however, are uniformly carved on stones by the roadsides. Continuing along the route of the Slea Head Drive, you'll see a signpost for Baile an Fheirtéaraigh (Ferriter's Town). In English it is called Ballyferriter. Michael Williams and Associates Architects' large modern building to your left, as you approach the village, houses the offices of Comharchumann Forbartha Chorca Dhuibhne and is the hub of its range of Irish-language-based courses, as well as pre-school and family support services, and provides facilities for local music, poetry and art festivals. In 2015 alone, the year of its opening, 2,500 students were due to attend courses there, injecting €7 million into the local economy.

On the right, just beyond the Comharchumann building, is Scoil Fheirtearaigh, the local national (primary) school. The village itself consists of a hotel and a church, several pubs, dwellings and shop premises, including a deli/café. The former national school building opposite the church on the main road now houses Músaem Chorca Dhuibhne, a beautifully curated regional museum. A road to the right, between the church and a shop, climbs up and around the side of Cruach Mhárthain to join The Clasach.

In the museum you can learn about the geology, archaeology, heritage and history of the area: it has a café, serving home baking, and a bookshop which also stocks cards and small gifts made in the area. Some of the artefacts on display in the museum are on loan from the National Museum of Ireland. Among the material held here is the extensive survey archive of Oidhreacht Chorca Dhuibhne's 1986 publication *The Archaeological Survey of the Dingle Peninsula*, by J. Cuppage *et al.*, and of *Flora Chorca Dhuibhne: Aspects of the Flora of Corca Dhuibhne* (Máirín Uí Chonchubhair/Aodán Ó Conchúir 1995), which can be seen by appointment. As well as caring for the museum's archive and its permanent exhibition, the curator works closely in conjunction with Oidhreacht Chorca Dhuibhne organising events and activities to promote aspects of the locality's intangible heritage with relation to Irish culture, and to promote the greater use of the Irish language.

The building is usually open seven days a week from 10.00 a.m. – 5.00 p.m. from June to mid-September. It also opens during the

Easter holiday season. Visits outside these dates can be arranged by phone, email or post: contact details can be found on the museum's informative website which is accessible in Irish, English, French, Spanish and German: www.westkerrymuseum.com

Entrance to Ballyferriter.

The Comharchumann Forbartha Chorca Dhuibhne building.

Músaem Chorca Dhuibhne, Ballyferriter's former national school.

Isabel Bennett

An archaeologist who was born in Wexford, Isabel is the curator of West Kerry Museum and lives near the Fahan Group of beehive huts where her husband's family have been answering tourists' questions about the area's history and heritage for generations.

❝ I first came to work for Oidhreacht Chorca Dhuibhne in the early 1980s. We were involved in the Archaeological Survey of Ireland which was established to compile an inventory of the known archaeological monuments in the state. At the time there were various archaeological exhibitions set up around the peninsula but there wasn't a museum. There was great concern at the time to have a local focus for heritage studies and preservation, and Oidhreacht Chorca Dhuibhne and the Comharchumann were the drivers. Then the old school building here in Ballyferriter became available for conversion because a new school was being built in the village. So an exhibition was established there that was running for several years with artefacts on loan from the National Museum in Dublin, including various artefacts from local excavations; and then, in 1993 or so, the loans policy for the national collection changed and the material on loan was to be returned because the conditions in which it was then kept weren't suitable. So the Comharchumann held meetings and sought advice and were told "if you employ a curator, if you improve security, if you upgrade the lighting and storage, and fulfil various other conditions, then we'd be happy to resume the loan". So they got a grant to employ someone for a year from the Heritage Council. And I applied for the position and got the job, and steps were taken to make the improvements, and the National Museum authorities were happy. So a formal loan arrangement was made, which is formally renewed at specific intervals. That's pretty remarkable for someplace of our size because not many museums that are not county museums would be deemed appropriate to house national artefacts. From then on we've continued to have a close relationship with the National Museum and we're involved with the Museum Standard Programme for Ireland which establishes levels of accreditation.

So, from the outset, the museum's establishment and continuation arose directly from the community and from local initiative. And the artefacts we have in it are directly related to the area, so when you're viewing the archaeological material, for example, you can go out the door into the countryside and see related sites. My job isn't a full-time one, and a lot of my time would be taken up grant-getting and form-filling, but as well as looking after the collection I deal directly with the public, which is great. I'd give talks, say, in the summer during Heritage Week. And people can come onto the museum's website and get the number to ring and make an appointment to come in when it's convenient – even out of season when the museum would be closed – and I can talk to them and show them what we have here.

There's always been a huge interest in what you can see around you in the landscape when you come here as a visitor, and it makes a big difference to people's enjoyment if you help them to see things in context. Like, we've developed a series of leaflets and maps here at the museum, with the routes of walks that start here and take you around a number of different sites. There are longish walks and shorter ones, so you can choose what suits you, and the leaflets are designed to be informative and easy to follow. We'd be talking about sites ranging from the prehistoric through to medieval and later ones and, if you know something about them before you get there, you can understand what you see, and see beyond it. It's fascinating, for example, if you know that Mediterranean pottery fragments were found at a particular monastic site to think of the monks' links with the outside world, and that monks here may have been importing their wine in amphorae. And if you're interested in Sybil Head because it was a setting for a *Star Wars* film, it adds a new dimension to know that the oldest settlement in Kerry – dated as early as 4,000 BC – was excavated just below that headland.

There's so much online these days as well. If you're here and you go away wanting to know more you should check the National Monuments Service site, www.archaeology.ie, which has the database for the Archaeological Survey. It covers the whole country but if you click on the database and pull in on the map, you'll see every site back here and information about each of them. Or search for the Ogham in 3D Project which is in the process of laser-scanning surviving ogham stones all across Ireland. You'll find stones there that were scanned only a mile or so from Músaem Chorca Dhuibhne, and when you come here you'll find them still standing or fallen in the exact places where they were first erected.

And, you know, you don't have to go off the beaten track to find things that are extraordinary. A Bronze Age standing stone, called Gallán na Cille Brice, is just there in the garden of a B&B that you pass on the road as you're driving west from Dingle. 〞

Ar oscailt 7 lá na seachtaine
Bealtaine – Méan Fómhair
Open 7 days, May – September

10.00 am – 5.30 pm

Deireadh Fómhair – Aibreán
Glaoigh 066-9156100
October – April by appointment

ABOVE: Músaem Chorca Dhuibhne's seasonal opening times are displayed on a plaque by the door.

LEFT: Músaem Chorca Dhuibhne interiors.

Ogham (pronounced *oh-am*) is the oldest-known form of writing in the Irish language and survives in carvings on standing stones, which were gravestones or territorial markers. The earliest examples may date from the end of the fourth century but the majority are from the fifth and sixth centuries, with some from the seventh century and even later. One third of Ireland's 350 or so known ogham stones are in County Kerry and more than sixty of these are located in southern and western parts of the Dingle Peninsula.

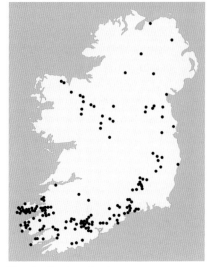

The distribution of ogham stones in Ireland.

Each stone carries the name of a male or males, with references to the individuals' ancestry. The name Dovinia is also present on several stones on the Dingle Peninsula: it is the Latin form of Duibhne, the ancient Celtic fertility goddess from whom the peninsula takes its name.

The legend of the fifth-century St Patrick's conversion of pagan Ireland simplifies the more complex history of the coming of Christianity and, despite the fact that the country was never colonised by Rome, there appears to have been a significant Roman presence in Ireland in the form of traders and possibly settlement. Most of the ogham stones on the peninsula are on sites that have connections to the Early Irish Christian Church. Many have crosses carved on them. It is possible that these were added at a later date than the ogham inscriptions; alternatively they may indicate a connection between ogham stones and the earliest pre-Patrician Church in the Munster area. Ogham inscriptions are also found in Wales, southwest England, the Isle of Man, and Scotland, including Shetland, and a single example in Silchester in southern England. The language of these inscriptions is predominantly Primitive Irish, apart from a few examples in Scotland, which record fragments of what is probably the Pictish language.

Músaem Chorca Dhuibhne has its own small, fascinating exhibition on ogham stones, including an interactive section where visitors can use a computer programme to write their own names in ogham script. It also has information about individual stones to be found in the area, and their locations.

Ballyferriter is named after the Anglo-Norman Feiritéar (Ferriter) family who settled in the area in the Late Medieval period. The older Irish name for the village, An Buailtín (variously translated as 'the flailing place' or 'the dung haggard'), is still used locally. The seventeenth-century poet Piaras Feiritéar is a local folk hero whose poetry lives on in the oral tradition. In 1641, during the period of unrest surrounding the English Civil War, Irish Catholic gentry who became known as the Confederates attempted to seize control of the English government administration in Ireland to force concessions for Catholics. The coup failed and there followed a period of ethnic conflict between native Irish Catholics on the one side, and English and Scottish Protestant settlers on the other. It was an attempt to establish who would govern Ireland, whether it would be governed from England, which ethnic and religious group would own most of the land, and which religion would predominate in the country. Ultimately, it was put down when the Confederate Catholics and their English Royalist allies were defeated during the Cromwellian conquest of Ireland (1649–53). The ruthlessness of Cromwell's campaign in Ireland is still vivid in folk memory. Feirtéar, who had been a leader on the Confederate side, was granted safe passage to arrange local surrender terms. However, he was seized at Castlemaine,

Ballyferriter is known locally as An Buailtín.

The rocky headland of Ceann Sibéal.

near the entrance to the Dingle Peninsula, and subsequently hanged in Killarney. According to folklore, the rope broke (which traditionally allowed the condemned man to go free) but the poet refused the reprieve, saying that he wouldn't have it said that he'd cheated death.

Feirtéar appears to have spoken English, as well as some French and Spanish. It has been suggested that he wrote poems in English as well as Irish, but only those in his native language survive. They include laments, eulogies, satires and love lyrics and, while largely written in the syllabic metre of the ancient Irish bardic tradition, some show evidence of European influence. In 2001, the Irish poet and writer Máire Mhac an tSaoi published an award-winning novella *A Bhean Óg Ón ...* (*O, Young Woman from ...*) about the supposed relationship between Feirtéar and the daughter of the English Earl of Bedford, for whom he is said to have written much of his love poetry.

Locally, Feirtéar is the subject of many legends of heroic prowess. In his book *The Western Island*, the scholar Robin Flower retells a story told to him by the islander Tomás Ó Criomhthain about the soldier poet taking refuge from his enemies on the Great Blasket: there are stories of his composing a poem in a cave there and of fighting off troops of Cromwellian soldiers single-handed. Ceann Sibéal, the headland that lies northwest of Ballyferriter village, is said to have been called after Feirtéar's wife. In 2016 it was used as a location for the eighth in the series of George Lucas' *Star Wars* films, in which mythological archetypes, similar to those recognised by George Thomson in Blasket Island storytelling, are combined with cinematic technology to turn old stories into new ones. Just as Dún Chaoin became 'the home of *Ryan's Daughter*', signs erected by locals in Ballyferriter proclaim it 'the home of *Star Wars*' and – as Isabel Bennett indicates above – visitor interest was, and continues to be, intense. During the *Star Wars* shoot a local video journalist interviewed Séamas Eoinín Feirtéar, a farmer who owns land near the site used for the filming. When asked what Piaras Feiritéar might have thought of the heroes of *Star Wars*, the modern-day Feirtéar was dismissive; he reckoned that, if it came to a fight, Piaras would beat the lot of them.

Scenes from the *Star Wars* film series were shot in spectacular locations near Ballyferriter in 2016.

Map outside Músaem Chorca Dhuibhne showing the routes of archaeological walks.

TIMELINE

The periods and ages commonly used to describe history and archaeology offer a helpful, if imprecise, way of understanding and conceiving of the passage of time; in reality there was considerable overlap in the characteristics used to define the different categories. No one knows exactly when habitation first occurred at the western end of the Dingle Peninsula but as you travel through the landscape it is useful to have a sense of the following timescale.

1 The Early Stone Age: Palaeolithic
(Cave dwellers) 50,000 BC to 9,000 BC.

2 The Middle Stone Age: Mesolithic
(Hunter-gatherers) 6000 BC onwards. Evidence of these inhabitants has been found on the Dingle Peninsula.

3 The Late Stone Age: Neolithic
(Farmers) c. 5000 BC. This was the beginning of the age of the standing stones and grave mounds and a time when the lowland areas were fairly extensively forested.

4 The Copper and Bronze Ages
(Traders) 2500–500 BC. Scholars disagree as to the date of the arrival of the Celts in Ireland. Some believe them to be associated with the Beaker People of the Bronze Age but it's more widely thought that they came later at the beginning of the Iron Age.

5 The Iron Age, 500 BC – AD 400
This was the time of hill forts and promontory forts and apparently a period of Pre-Christian cultural expansion and consolidation.

6 The Early Medieval Period, AD 400–1200
The period of Early Christian expansion, when sites such as the Fahan (beehive huts) Group and the medieval monastic settlements and pilgrimage routes were established, and ogham stones began to be erected.

7 From the English Invasion of Ireland, AD 1200, to the present day

The Anglo-Norman conquest was followed by a period of conflict between the colonial settlers and the sixteenth-century Post-Reformation Tudor administration in England. This ended with the re-establishment of English control and, by the late seventeenth century, the destruction of all that had survived of the old Gaelic order. Thereafter the English administration suppressed native Irish culture and political, social, economic and religious freedom and much of the social order conformed or responded to the English model. Several centuries of sporadic rebellion in Ireland followed. The eighteenth century was marked by rural agitation against the Anglo-Irish landlords. Devastating famine in the nineteenth century led to widespread emigration at the same time as a new nationalist movement was kindled at home. The 1916 Rising signalled the end to British rule in Ireland. It was followed by the War of Independence (1919–1921), a brief and bitter civil war and the subsequent formal establishment of a Free State (1922) and then a Republic (1948) in twenty-six of the island's thirty-two counties. The Republic of Ireland joined the European Union (then the EEC) in 1973.

Deserted cottage near Ballyferriter, on the slopes of Cruach Mhárthain.

9 Around Riasc

Béal Bán beach.

THE FIRST TURN to your left as you drive out of Baile an Fheirtéaraigh leads down a narrow, winding road to Béal Bán. The name of this beautiful beach, which is a favourite local destination for walking and bathing, translates as 'The White Mouth'. Here local members of the Irish Volunteers, armed with the help of The O'Rahilly, trained for months in the run-up to the 1916 Rising. On 22 April 1916 – in advance of the taking of the General Post Office in Dublin on 24 April – over a hundred Volunteers from the Dingle Peninsula took part in a night march across the Conor Pass. Their mission, though at the time they were unaware of it, was to liaise with Roger Casement, a leader of the Rising who was bringing a consignment of arms from Germany. The weather was bad and the road worse and many of the men reached Tralee barefoot.

In the event, Casement was captured, the ship with its cargo of arms was scuttled and Robert Monteith, who had accompanied Casement from Germany, brought the news to Tralee where the men of the west were stood down. It was the loss of these arms that precipitated the order to postpone the rising, which The O'Rahilly travelled the country to deliver before returning to Dublin and throwing in his lot with the ill-fated rebels who rose on Easter Monday.

When one of the men who set out to cross the Conor Pass was warned that he might not return he replied philosophically: *'más é ár lá é, 'sé ár lá é'* ('if it's our day, it's our day').

Béal Bán, seen here in February, is a popular beach for walking throughout the year.

Gathering in Baile an Fheirtéaraigh, 22 April 2016. The replica rifles were made by a local carpenter.

Mary Sheehy ('Mold') in old age.
COURTESY GEARÓID MAC AN tSÍTHIGH

In the 1960s personal statements were collected from surviving Gaeltacht participants in the march, all of whom had set out assuming they were going into action. They tell an extraordinary story of courage and physical resilience. Among them is one from Paddy Martin, known as An Mairtíneach, who remarks, almost in passing, that he and a companion undertook the 60km trek to Tralee having had no sleep the previous night, because they had been out at sea, fishing.

The march is commemorated in a painting by Liam O'Neill, who was born and lives in Corca Dhuibhne and is one of Ireland's foremost contemporary artists. An exhibition of O'Neill's works travelled to New York in May 2016 as part of the 1916 Rising Centenary commemorations; his painting depicting the march from Baile an Fheirtéaraigh is reproduced on the reverse of the bottles containing the Dingle Whiskey Distillery's first batch of whiskey, issued in November 2016.

On 22 April 2016 members of the families of local men who made the night march across the Conor Pass re-enacted it on foot, starting from Baile an Fheirtéaraigh. They were accompanied by local women and girls and others and, having marched through the night, were played into Tralee by pipers, in commemoration of musicians from the town who met the original march. The replica rifles were made by a local carpenter. Among those who gathered in Baile an Fheirtéaraigh to see the 2016 marchers off was a nephew of Mary Sheehy of Baile Eaglaise (Church Town), who was only in her teens when she joined Cumann na mBan, inspired by the 1916 Rising. During the War of Independence, Mary and other Cumann na mBan members in the area acted as couriers and as a network of support for their male companions in arms. Her nephew Gearóid Mac an tSíthigh attended the event wearing her medals, saying he was there to make sure that his late aunt's involvement in the struggle for independence was remembered.

Béal Bán beach is also the location of annual midsummer horse racing, a recently revived tradition that reaches back to seasonal festivities associated with the Celtic feast of Lughnasa which celebrated the harvest sun-god Lugh.

Farther down the road, at the entrance to a lane on the left, is a memorial to Tomás Ó Suilleabháin, a young man from the nearby village of Baile an Éanaigh, (possibly 'Market Town') who died fighting in the civil war (1922–1923) that followed the War of Independence. The memory of the civil war is still painful in Ireland and it is seldom spoken of, particularly in small and isolated communities where families and neighbours who had fought shoulder to shoulder only months before often took separate sides.

Horse racing on Béal Bán beach.

CONVERSATION:
Cathy Corduff

Cathy Corduff, who was born in Baile an Éanaigh, spent much of her adult life living and working in Springfield, Massachusetts. In the 1970s she and her husband returned to live in the house where she was born, and one of her sons is now raising a family nearby.

❝ When I went over I had no notion of how long I'd stay in America. I went for my brother's wedding in Springfield in 1964 and I thought "what am I doing at home?" There were no jobs round here. I was a children's nurse and I worked in Cork and Tralee. And I'd met my husband Christy at my brother's wedding and I liked him, so I thought I'd go back over. I remember I met the priest when I came home from that wedding and I told him and he said "*Duine eile imithe*" [another person gone]. That's what he said.

I was very lonely, though, when I first went over because I missed my friends here. And I used to love to come home. My aunt and my father never wanted me to go back. But when you came out of church in Our Lady of Hope church in Springfield it was like being at home. All the Ventry people that were there, and all the people from all around. And all speaking Irish. My brother to this day, and he's over sixty years in the States, speaks Irish. As if he never left here. And I had a load of family over there – two uncles and a cousin and my aunt and more – and I worked in Shriners Hospital for crippled children and there was even a nurse there who'd been to school with my mother.

My mother died when I was born. The banshee cried for her the week before. That's what my uncle said. He was coming past the graveyard late at night with a friend and they heard keening in the graveyard. And when I was born my mother died and I was sent to my aunt who lived with my grandmother in Gallarus. And when she married into Baile Uachtarach she took me with her.

Farmland near Baile an Éanaigh.

I was the only child growing up there and I loved it because all the old ladies were so good to me. So, though Baile an Éanaigh was where I was born, it took me a long time to settle down here when Christy and I came home in the 1970s. I was pregnant coming home from the States too, which made it worse. But, you know I wouldn't live in the States now if they gave me all the dollars in the world. It's all go, go, go, work, work, work. One of my own sons is there now and coming home is his big thing. Looking forward to coming home. He loves it there but, my God, he works!

This is a better place to rear a family. In the States, you couldn't take your eyes off them. Where we lived there we had a little pool in the garden and I used to leave the kids out to play and maybe go upstairs myself. And my neighbour said to me, "I don't see you with the kids," she said. "Come down to them. They could be nicked." My God, I almost died. But when I came back here to live, the relief of leaving them out, and they'd jump the ditch over to my neighbour Peggy and they'd be fine. You're more relaxed here. You kind of go slow when you come here.

When I was young we used to cycle to all the dances. Only I used to be terrified coming home in the night and cycling past

The Dingle Peninsula's mild climate is the result of the effect of the Gulf Stream.

the graveyard. And it's worse I'm getting now that I'm older! I'm afraid of *púcaí* [ghosts]. Years ago, the local lads here knew that, and one night they put a lighted candle in a jam jar at the entrance to the graveyard. I was nearly dead of fright by the time I got home. You'd be afraid of spirits and ghosts and fairies, but you'd have to keep going if you wanted to get home to your bed. I was coming home with a friend one time and we saw two women with scarves over their heads going past in the dark of the night. My God, I thought they were from the other world. We had great fun when I was a teenager, though; we had a great life altogether.

My other son was in America for a while and he couldn't wait to come home. Loves to visit but can't wait to come back. He prefers the life here and he'd be lonely when he's away. Christy and I are married fifty years next year and we might go over ourselves to visit. My son there asked would we not come over this year and I said no. "We're too old at the moment," I told him, "we might be younger next year." The thing is, I never did like the heat. I'd prefer the weather here.

I loved Springfield, though. Every second door was Irish. And I loved the shopping – that's the one thing I missed when I came

Modern farm walls are often built using traditional skills.

away. And still when I go over and I go shopping I walk in the door of a store and I get goosebumps. I love it. But the houses here are better now than the houses over in America. They weren't long ago, but they're way better now. Beautiful homes here now, fine houses.

This place has come on so much in the last thirty years or so. I suppose it was *Ryan's Daughter* and they got money, and they'd build a house, and they got to work, and they got more prosperous. And they got a better education. And back in Baile Uachtarach now – I'd go back there sometimes to where I grew up – and there are all sorts of sheds there that were my uncle's, and they've been bought up and developed since – the outhouses, the cow house, the hayshed – and I look at them now and I say to myself "I used to milk cows in these sheds." "A century ago," I say to myself, "they're very nice but there's so many memories …" The only thing that's left is the henhouse. They didn't touch the henhouse.

But I don't miss that life at all. It was very hard. In those days you milked by hand. My aunt's husband was the first to have a milking machine in Baile Uachtarach. My aunt ever hated to milk cows with a milking machine but I used to do it. And up to this day I'd be very interested in watching. I look at the new machines and I'm interested. Milking so many cows together. My God, it's unbelievable.

This shed back west, now used as a henhouse, was formerly a dwelling.

But it's gone from here now. The day of milking of the cows is over or there's only a few milking. Because the creamery is gone. Christy used to tell my father years ago, "the day of the white coat is coming to the cow house." My father thought he was nuts. Now it's come. All the tests and it all has to be perfect. But now they're saying too that it was how things were that gave us a strong immune system. My aunt had two cows – I don't know was it two or three – and she had a churn and she used to have cream for everyone, buttermilk for everyone. We'd have to stop at every house to give it in to people whenever we drove into Dingle. It was cream for this one, buttermilk for that one – I used to say to her, "I wish you'd sell those cows! I don't want to be stopping on the road every minute and I going to Dingle!" And she was forever baking; she'd never buy a cake because she'd make them. She made butter all the time. She'd always have a pie on the table.

She was so generous, my aunt! And the Yanks are like that. The people in America, they'd drive for miles to take you somewhere, and their doors would always be open. They couldn't do too much for you. I wouldn't live there now myself but I love the connection. I love the thought that my family has roots in the two places.

Until comparatively recently farmers here would take milk to their local creamery to sell, and the closure of the last of these focal points in the community marked a turning point in the history of the area. The creamery that was nearest to Baile an Éanaigh now stands boarded up on the turn of the road before Brick's pub, having finally closed in 2006, and visitors staying in the pub's B&B accommodation, or taking a tour of its microbrewery, hardly notice it. The brewery, established by the pub's owners in 2008, now supplies award-winning hand-crafted and artisan beers throughout the peninsula. From this point on the Slea Head Drive you'll find only one hotel but there are many charming, comfortable places to get B&B or guesthouse accommodation; information about them can be had from the tourist office in Dingle, as well as online and if, when you're driving back west, you find yourself wanting to spend more time in a particular location, it's always worth knocking at the door of a B&B and asking for a room or suggestions for where to find one.

Beyond Brick's, which was built in the 1890s, is the turn to An Riasc (The Marsh), one of the area's most striking medieval monastic sites, which has an elaborately carved cross slab inscribed with Classical, Celtic and Christian motifs. There are about sixty medieval ecclesiastical sites on the Dingle Peninsula, ten of which are monastic settlements concentrated within a few kilometres of each other in the landscape beyond Baile an Fheirtéaraigh. Their presence within such a small area suggests that the western end of the peninsula was a significant centre for the introduction and development of the

Medieval monastic site at An Riasc overlooking Smerwick Harbour.

Cross slab at An Riasc.

Early Christian Church in the period between the fifth and sixth centuries. The remains at An Riasc give no more than a tranquil impression in a grassy field of the busy network of buildings that once housed a religious community there: others, such as the ruins of the Romanesque church at Cill Mhaoil Chéadair (the graveyard/church of Malkedar) or the remarkable oratory at Gall Ioros are more intact. The name of the oratory has variously been

The west façade of the ruined medieval church at Cill Mhaoil Chéadair (Kilmalkedar).

Detail of coloured stone.

Romanesque window, Cill Mhaoil Chéadair church interior.

Cill Mhaoil Chéadair churchyard.

Standing stone at Gallarus Oratory.

The splayed base of the walls of Gallarus Oratory supports the corbelled arch of the roof.

translated as 'rocky headland/ peninsula' or 'the shelter/ peninsula of foreigners', the latter suggesting that it could have been, or been near, a pilgrim rest house. Its English language name 'Gallarus Oratory' tends to be used locally. When visiting ecclesiastical sites, do remember that some, including Gallarus Oratory, and especially those with surrounding graveyards, are still used on occasion for religious services and should be treated with the same degree of respect that you'd give to any place of worship.

The word 'monk', which derives from the Greek, means 'single' or 'solitary'. In its original language it can apply both to men and women, though in English it came to mean men only, with 'nun' being used to describe a female religious. Early Christian monks and nuns followed the eremitic or cenobitic traditions, choosing either a life of isolation and seclusion or of communal discipline. The eremitic tradition was the earlier of the two but there is evidence that, as time went on, both flourished simultaneously. Typically, monastic communities relied on grants of land from local chieftains who had embraced or tolerated Christianity. The monks responded by offering pastoral, and often medical, care to the local population, and may also have offered hostel accommodation to medieval

ABOVE: The ruins of Rahinnane Castle.
RIGHT: The restored Gallarus Castle.

pilgrims. So, while it is possible that Early Christian churchmen and women came to this area because of its remote location, it is equally likely that its attraction lay in the fact that at the time it was a centre of secular authority, and widely populated. Many of the monastic sites in the area have been excavated, with incidences of preservation and restoration work clearly indicated and explained on information boards.

The museum in Ballyferriter has a series of leaflets containing maps of walks to local historic and prehistoric archaeological sites, and information about them, presented both in Irish and English and commissioned by Oidhreacht Chorca Dhuibhne. The sites covered range from the earliest times through the arrival of the Corcu Duibhne and the peninsula's other named inhabitants, the Ciarraighe and the Gaels (1500 BC – AD 400), to the first Christian presence (AD 400–1100), the invasions of the Danes and the Normans (AD 800–1600) and the Anglo-Irish presence on the peninsula. They include two 'castles' – Gallarus and Rahinnane – which are fortified tower houses of a type typical in Ireland. Rahinnane Castle is called *Ráth Sheanáin* in Irish, which translates as 'Senan's Fort'. Built on the site of a prehistoric fort, it probably dates from the fifteenth century and the site itself may have been occupied continuously from the Iron Age (500 BC – AD 400) to the seventeenth-century Cromwellian wars. The castle was the stronghold of the Anglo-Norman Fitzgeralds, Knights of Kerry, and was destroyed by Cromwell's soldiers, though the family remained

The Saints' Road takes walkers through some of the most beautiful scenery on the Dingle Peninsula.

in residence at the site until the early eighteenth century. The outline of the earlier ring fort that surrounds the ruins of the fifteenth-century castle is clearly visible, particularly in evening light. Gallarus Castle, also a Fitzgerald stronghold and dating from the same period, is in a better state of preservation than Rahinnane. There is no record of its having been destroyed in war, but it was used in Cromwellian times, and for garrisoning troops during the siege of Dún an Óir . It is a four-storey structure, originally accessed on the first floor, and retains its vaulted roof. A two-storey defensive structure to the front is now gone but evidence of it can be seen on the external wall.

Músaem Chorca Dhuibhne also offers information about pilgrimage routes in the area: the 18km pilgrims' path from Ventry Strand to the foot of Mount Brandon known as 'The Saints' Road' is now incorporated into the Dingle Way, a 162km-long circular hiking route that begins and ends in Tralee.

We do not know what the first settlers on the peninsula called themselves and no indications of their dwellings survive, but their tombs and inscribed stones remain to bear witness to their presence. Over time these tombs became associated in folklore with the Tuatha Dé Danann, a name which, like Corcu Duibhne, translates as 'the people of the goddess Danu': it also occasionally appears as the Tuatha Dé, 'the people of the gods'. This was a supernatural race believed to live in an underground Otherworld, having retreated from the human world which it continued to visit and affect. It is likely that the belief arose from a race memory of early inhabitants who had literally 'gone into the mounds' that covered their tombs, so that the fact of the mounds as gravesites became subsumed by the myth of them as portals to an Otherworld. One result of this belief was the survival of the tombs across millennia because of an inherited superstition that tampering with them would provoke the anger of the Tuatha Dé.

So, like the modern graveyards that frightened the teenaged Cathy Corduff as she cycled home from dances, prehistoric grave mounds were avoided as the haunts of *púcaí*. This sense of awareness of the continued presence of the spirits of the dead within the community still appears in local folklore. For example, the most recently interred body in a modern graveyard is said to walk nightly to the nearest stream or well to draw water for the other corpses buried there, and to cross *Bóthar na Marbh* (The Road of the Dead), as the notional path is known, is to risk meeting his or her ghost.

The fairies, Good People or Little People of Irish folklore emerged from the belief in the Tuatha Dé Danann and – unlike the butterfly-winged idea of fairies that arose from those depicted in Shakespeare's *A Midsummer Night's Dream* – their origins are rooted in an atavistic fear of, and respect for, the dead. The idea of the Banshee – from '*Bean Sídhe*' which means 'fairy woman' – arises from the folk tradition that a race known as the *Sídhe* who, in some instances, are also identified with the Tuatha Dé, inhabit 'fairy hills' throughout Ireland: their name in Irish '*Aos Sí*', from the older form *Aes Sidhe*, literally means 'the people of the mounds'.

In the past it was also believed that the circular mounds covering prehistoric tombs were gathering places where fairies would dance, and that lone trees and bushes in the landscape marked entrances

A lone furze bush near Gallarus.

to their dwellings. To spy on them or disturb them was considered dangerous, and the fairies' revenge might include cursing cattle to dry up their milk or burning down hay sheds and houses. It was said that women were abducted and imprisoned in 'fairy mounds' and that babies taken there from their cradles were replaced with sickly fairy children. In most stories it is possible to recover the woman or the child stolen by the fairies through courage or cunning, though often the attempt goes wrong: the belief probably represented imaginative explanations of, and responses to, the loss of mothers in childbirth, and of infant mortality.

When travellers took the emigrant road, folklore and traditions travelled with them.

Many folk beliefs travelled with emigrants to America and elsewhere and morphed into modern customs and festivities. Halloween festivities, for example, which probably came to North America from the British Isles at the beginning of the nineteenth century, spread widely through the United States with the arrival of large numbers of Irish immigrants after the Great Famine. The festival's origin in the pre-Christian Celtic belief that the veil between this world and the Otherworld is thinnest at seasonal turning points has been questioned by some scholars, but undoubtedly it belongs to the tradition that returning spirits of benign ancestors should be propitiated with gifts of food, while angry spirits could be warded off with ritual aggression.

EMIGRATION

About 33.3 million Americans – 10.5 per cent of the total population – reported Irish ancestry in a 2013 survey conducted by the US Census Bureau (compare this with a population of about 6.4 million in Ireland, north and south). Migrants brought the Irish language with them to North America as early as the seventeenth century, when it was still in widespread use across the whole island of Ireland.

Cathy and Christy Corduff's wedding photo, taken in a studio in Springfield, Massachusetts.
COURTESY CATHY CORDUFF

Immigrants the world over tend to congregate in specific areas of their new countries, usually settling where family members have settled and found employment before them. Until very recently Hartford, in Connecticut, and the Springfield and Holyoak areas of Massachusetts were the most common destinations for people emigrating from the end of the Dingle Peninsula to the US.

As late as 1795, nearly 95 per cent of the population of Massachusetts was of English ancestry but during the early and mid-nineteenth century, immigrant groups from Ireland began arriving in large numbers. Many arrived in the 1840s fleeing the potato famine, and a high percentage came from areas along the western seaboard where, although it had diminished in other parts of Ireland, Irish was still the first language. Even now in Holyoak and Springfield, and in Hartford, Connecticut, you can hear Irish spoken with the pure idiom and accent of specific areas back west.

Today five of the top twenty counties in the USA with the greatest percentage of speakers of Irish are located in New York and Massachusetts, while the Irish and part-Irish are the largest ancestry group in the state of Massachusetts at nearly 25 per cent of the total population.

In the twenty-first century, people from back west often choose Canada or Australia when emigrating for work. There too they find evidence of Ireland's widespread cultural diaspora. In all, 1.2 million Irish immigrants arrived in Canada from 1825 to 1970, at least half of those between 1831 and 1850. By 1867, they were Canada's second-largest ethnic group (after the French), and comprised 24 per cent of the population, many of whom still spoke Irish. The language reached Australia in 1788, along with English, and was widely used by convicts in the early colonial period. By the late nineteenth century, about a third of the population in Australia was Irish, and today the University of Melbourne houses a remarkable and valuable collection of nineteenth- and early twentieth-century books and manuscripts in the Irish language.

Béal Bán beach.

10 Ballydavid

Ballydavid and Smerwick Harbour.
INSET: Ballydavid Pier.

Winter sunset behind Cruach Mhárthain from Cill Mhaoil Chéadair.

AS YOU CONTINUE along the route of the Slea Head Drive you approach the least-travelled region west of Dingle town. Two of the greatest pleasures to be found here are peace and spectacular scenery. There are idyllic clifftop and mountain walks, beaches and long narrow roads to wander, the quality of the light makes it a paradise for artists and photographers, and all through the year you can enjoy breathtaking sunsets over the Atlantic.

While this part of the west has few cafés or overt commercial tourist attractions, there are shops that will sell you the makings of a picnic, and pubs where tea, coffee and sandwiches are served as well as alcohol and, in some cases, full meals. Chowder and seafood are specialities of the area, as is brown soda bread; and the white-bread sandwich known as a 'toasted special', usually filled with ham, cheese, tomato and onion, makes a satisfying lunch.

Talking to bar staff and local people, you may discover where to go to hear traditional music in the evenings – not sessions organised for tourists, but neighbours and friends coming together in a pub to play for their own entertainment. The village of Baile na nGall, referred to in English as Ballydavid, has two pubs, both of which often attract local musicians in the evenings. In good weather you can sit outdoors with your pint or your food overlooking a small, sandy beach bisected by a little pier, with glorious views of Smerwick

The pier at Baile na nGall.

Harbour. The name of the village translates as 'the town of the foreigners', and may indicate the presence of a Viking settlement in the locality, given the derivation of 'Smerwick' from the Norse words for 'butter harbour'.

A 'thank you' sign in Irish at one of the pier head pubs in Baile na nGall.

Sign for Ard na Caithne with a trail marker beside it.

The area on the far side of the harbour, which appears on some maps as Smerwick, is now officially known by its Irish name Ard na Caithne (the high place of the arbutus). The arbutus, or Strawberry tree, is a small tree or shrub with edible red berries. If arbutus flourished widely here in the past, the view must have been even more striking than it is now; the flowers appear while the previous year's fruit are ripening, as fruit development is delayed for about five months after pollination. Today the landscape consists

Second World War lookout post near Baile na nGall.

of green fields, small groups of farm buildings and dwellings, and windswept outcrops of rock patterned with extraordinarily vibrant patches of coloured lichen.

Walking north along the cliffs in Baile na nGall you will see the remains of a lookout post, one of many set up around the neutral Irish coastline during the Second World War.

Beyond the village of Baile na nGall is the tall mast on the cliffs that pinpoints the presence of the Corca Dhuibhne studios of Ireland's Irish-language radio station, Raidió na Gaeltachta. The genesis of the station, which celebrated its fortieth anniversary in 2012, is another example of the Gaeltacht areas' history of local effort and enterprise.

From 1968 onwards, a Gaeltacht Civil Rights Movement began calling for a broad list of improvements in education, fishing rights and the provision of communications. Branches were set up in Connemara and Corca Dhuibhne and the Dublin-based Irish-language publishing house Sáirséal agus Dill trained printers to produce a newspaper for the movement. Within two years further national attention was also drawn to Gaeltacht civil rights by the march to Dublin in protest against the closure of Scoil Naomh Gobnait in Dún Chaoin. With continued assistance from Sáirséal agus Dill and other well-wishers, and from Michael Healy, a young engineer from Cork, the Gaeltacht Civil Rights Movement set up a pirate station in Ros Muc, Connemara, where its first broadcast was

Green and white lichen on rocks near Ard na Caithne.

made at Easter 1970. Wide local audiences achieved by the pirate station and increasing pressure nationwide led to the establishment of Raidió na Gaeltachta as the Irish-language radio service of the national public-service broadcaster RTÉ. The official station began broadcasting from its main studio at Casla in Connemara on Easter Sunday, 2 April 1972.

Initially, Raidió na Gaeltachta broadcast for a few hours a day and was only available in or near the three largest Gaeltacht areas. It is now available on FM in Ireland and via satellite and on the Internet (www.rte.ie/rnag). It broadcasts news, sports, magazine and music programmes from studios in Gaoth Dobhair (Gweedore), County Donegal; Baile na nGall in Corca Dhuibhne; Castlebar, County Mayo,

Raidió na Gaeltachta's output serves both regional and national audiences.

and also has studios in Rinn Ó gCuanach, County Waterford, and the RTÉ Radio Centre in Dublin. The output is entirely in Irish but there is a high quantity of music content, so tuning in can make an interesting background to your experience of the area. For those who read Irish, the detailed and beautifully illustrated history of the publishing house, *Sáirséal Agus Dill 1947 – 1981 Scéal Foilsitheora,* (The Story of a Publisher) (Cló Iar-Chonnacht 2014), by Cian Ó hÉigeartaigh and Corca Dhuibhne resident Aoileann Nic Gearailt, provides what amounts to a historical overview of Irish-language publishing in the Republic between those dates.

CONVERSATION:
Dara Ó Cinnéide, Raidió Na Gaeltachta

Dara Ó Cinnéide produces *An Saol Ó Dheas* **(***Life Back West***), a Monday–Friday magazine programme broadcast from the station's Baile na nGall studios. A national Gaelic football hero who was born and raised in the area, he played with his local club An Ghaeltacht and was a member of the Kerry senior inter-county team from 1995 until 2005. In 2004 he captained Kerry to the All-Ireland title and he continues to coach for the Gaeltacht team.**

❝ I suppose most young people raised round here don't really think of the language in terms of an inheritance. It's just a means of communication. But when I went away at the age of about eighteen – I had seven years in Limerick studying chemistry and education – I realised I had something here and I wasn't utilising it. I needed to get back, and I made a decision at the age of twenty-four or twenty-five that I wanted to be living and working in this area. I wanted to travel as much as I could but the base was always going to be Baile na hAbha [The Town of the River] at the foot of Mount Brandon.

I was looking for jobs – obviously there were no chemistry or teaching jobs round here – and I got a part time job here in Raidió na Gaeltachta in my last year in college, and found that I was learning something every day – new ways of saying things, correct ways of saying things, different ways of saying things. Obviously, there are days when you're just feeding the machine, because it's news, current affairs and reporting on events. But more times you're actually going into communities and meeting people and hearing their stories and their songs. Getting to know different Gaeltacht areas, in the Munster region in particular, is what drew me in. And going into the archive here and just being blown away by what's in there. Most of my day is spent looking forward, as opposed to looking back forty years or so to the founding of this organisation, so even after seventeen years working here I haven't had time to get through all of what's in the archive. But that was what intrigued me to begin with. And I was learning from people working here who had such a knowledge of the language and who'd draw my attention to grammatical nuances I'd never even known about – nobody my age did. I would have been offered other jobs in Dublin and places but they weren't for me because after a year or two of this I just didn't want to be anywhere else.

In the archive there are recordings of people that didn't hear English at all when they were young. We've four kids ourselves at home now and we rear them through the Irish language, but it's a different language nowadays. Most of the people we'd deal with on an everyday basis are bilingual or multilingual but, when Raidió na Gaeltachta started off, the voices being recorded were almost exclusively those of people who only had Irish. Somebody once said that when society is seen to break down, sociology emerges as a discipline. That's the kind of worry I'd have for our language, that people see it as being codified before it goes out of existence, almost. And to some degree that is what Raidió na Gaeltachta does, we're part of that process, and in one way that's something I lament. But in another way I'm proud to be part of it. Our standards and our journalism would be exactly the same as the English-language broadcasters, but a big part of what we do would be about preserving what's here in this place.

The mast at Raidió na Gaeltachta's Corca Dhuibhne studios, viewed here from Ard na Caithne, is dwarfed by Mount Brandon.

There's a debate raging still about the standardisation of the language, and whether it's a good thing and whether it undermines the richness of the language of the people. And that's a big concern for the broadcasters. But, then again, that's not unique to Irish. I'd say if you went to France you'd find Corsicans having the same discussion, and you'd find it elsewhere in the world.

One of Raidió na Gaeltachta's major contributions to the language in the early years – the 1970s – was the breakdown of barriers between the different dialects, and even the different Gaeltacht communities. Now we've moved on and we hardly remember that, but in the beginning people were most interested in programmes broadcast from their own region because that was their Irish and they understood it. So that's what they listened to. But then, maybe, they'd leave the radio on in the background when something was being broadcast by the Donegal crowd or Connemara crowd, and quite quickly they began to say to themselves "yes, I can understand what they're saying, and I do get them and where they're coming from." I had the same experience myself about ten years ago when I was coaching Gaelic football to a bunch of kids in the Donegal Gaeltacht. I was a guest there barking out instructions and I was able to adjust and give them a certain amount in their own dialect, and that made a difference. I wouldn't have been able to do that had I not grown up listening to Raidió na Gaeltachta.

I suppose Raidió na Gaeltachta was the embodiment of the notion that you could have a community that embraced all the Gaeltacht areas, and that all that was different was the nuances. There's a common language there and that's the identifier. When I came here to the station first I remember talking about the "Gaeltachataí", which is the plural in Irish, and I remember being asked "why do you say Gaeltachtaí? It's 'the Gaeltacht'." And it is. I think I'd describe myself as a Gaeltacht person rather than a Kerry person, and I'd identify more with another Munster Gaeltacht – say An Rinn in Waterford – than I would with places in my own county where they wouldn't speak Irish. That mightn't always be the popular thing to say when you're wearing a Kerry jersey on the football field but it's very deeply embedded, that sense of being from the Gaeltacht first and foremost. You might switch on the radio and hear that the fishermen in Connemara

Autumnal view of the pier at Baile na nGall
stretching into Smerwick Harbour.

INSET: A small stack of fish boxes in Baile na nGall.

are having trouble, say, and you'd say "d'you know, we had the same trouble ourselves a few years ago" – because of the peripherality of it and because of the nature of the work done along the Atlantic seaboard, a lot of the troubles and the problems are common. The village here once supported a thriving fishing community. It's even the case that dialects within dialects can be lost, and there can be a negative cultural effect, because of economic policies that affect traditional ways of living. Some of the richness of the language was just swept away with the loss of local fishing communities. That particular richness is gone round here and it's gone forever.

But it's about place as well as language. When I'm coaching the kids here, they're playing in a field in a landscape that belongs to them. It's their heritage. The other thing people talk about now is the idea of the "Online Gaeltacht" – that it exists in cyberspace. I would rail against that because we have something real here in the real world that we've managed to preserve. It's

Training times posted at Gallarus playing field.

living and breathing, and it's here. Let all the students in the world draw from that well if they want to, but while we're still here raising our kids through Irish, sending them to school here, the Gaeltacht is a physical place, and that's important.

Over the last twenty to twenty-five years we've had Lithuanians and Latvians and Poles coming here and working here and I think that's had a good effect. I think people have heard them speaking their own languages and it's dawned on them "yes, we have our own language too and why wouldn't we speak it?" Really it's just a rainbow and we want to preserve our colour within that rainbow, without impinging upon anybody else. But the different colours are distinct and that's important. We're all willing to embrace all cultures coming in, but there has to be recognition that this is a Gaeltacht area. We don't want to be battling all the time, but, when there are battles to fight, it very much comes from the heart. It means a lot to those of us who want to hand on the traditions that were handed down to us.

What gives us most encouragement is people who come in from the outside and recognise what's here. Sometimes I think it's Gaeltacht people themselves who don't recognise the value of it. The truth is that the biggest tourist attraction here is the culture and the language. It always has been. If I wanted one thing for us it would be a greater and an explicit acknowledgement of that. But people here have something – I don't know if it's maybe just courtesy and politeness – that makes us speak English even if there's only one person sitting

Baile na nGall viewed across the broad expanse of Smerwick Harbour.

around the table with us that doesn't have Irish. And it happens even when that one person would love to hear Irish spoken and would see it as an important part of the experience of being here. When Raidió na Gaeltachta started it was the main means of mass communication for people in the Gaeltacht. That's changed now because of the Internet and social media so, in a way, it's harder now to gauge the effect of our impact. Our core demographic isn't likely to be tweeting about what they're listening to but, on the other hand, quite a high proportion of the voices you'd hear in our programmes would also be members of our audience. That's a level of engagement with the local community that we really try to foster. For me, the best radio is somebody talking about something that happens, and it doesn't just have to be something that's happening round here. You're balancing all the time – getting the right balance between local interest and global interest. And finding people with engaging stories to tell.

We podcast and we get good reactions to that, and the extent of the downloading is monitored. Now, some of our online audience interest would be academic – people interested in the language, not the stories. But we're always trying to broadcast

Plaque commemorating names of fishermen lost at sea, Ard na Caithne.
Shared memory of local history is a vital part of the Gaeltacht heritage.

content that would be relevant in itself, and we're looking at a
very wide audience. You might have an elderly person who finds
comfort in tunes that they knew from the past, but you're also
thinking about the twenty-year-old from the locality who's gone
off to university, say, in Limerick or in Galway. What are we doing
for them? Now, I'm not sure I listened all that much to Raidió na
Gaeltachta myself at that age, but they're our next group of adults
and parents, say, in ten years' time, so they're a major challenge.

When I was playing football, just to get into the right state of
relaxation before going out and playing in front of a thousand
people, I'd go into my father's fields in my mind, into all the places
I know here, along the cliffs and into the mountains. Cuas an
Bhodaigh [The Churl's Creek] and up along there would be my
father's land. I'd go into that landscape. That's what defines me.
The landscape and the language.

As well as producing for Raidió na Gaeltachta, Ó Cinnéide is a TV panellist and journalist and for eleven years presented the main sports show for Ireland's Irish-language TV station. The history of that station, launched on 31 October 1996, also began in the Gaeltacht and arose from the same grassroots impetus that fuelled the Gaeltacht Civil Rights Movement.

The channel, initially known as Teilifís na Gaeilge, was rebranded in 1999 as TG4. It is available to 98 per cent of homes in Ireland. It is also available internationally through the TG4 Player (www. tg4.ie/en/player/home).

The dedicated Irish-language station emerged from a pirate enterprise called Telefís na Gaeltachta, set up in Connemara in 1987 and broadcast from a transmitter paid for by donations from Gaeltacht communities. As with Raidió na Gaeltachta, local and national pressure led to the adoption of the idea by central government, and Michael D. Higgins – later president of Ireland, then Minister for Arts, Culture and the Gaeltacht – was made responsible for the establishment and launch of the official station. In 2007 TG4 became independent from RTÉ, from which it still receives significant assistance in non-monetary terms, and became a member of the European Broadcasting Union. In 2008 it became a founding member of the World Indigenous Television Broadcasters Network, the members of which include New Zealand's Maori, Norway and Finland's Sámi, and the USA's First Nation's radio and television stations.

To a certain extent, TV and radio broadcasts of music from local pubs, area-specific newscasting and daily listings of community information, ranging from sporting fixtures to deaths and funeral notices, have filled a gap left by the loss of the custom of *bothántaíocht*. *Bothán* means a little house or cabin and *bothántaíocht* means to go visiting, or join a gathering, in a neighbour's house. Irish-language television has become a vital resource for Gaeltacht communities. In the past certain houses became centres for *bothántaíocht* because of their position, reputation for hospitality, or because they were the homes of recognised musicians or storytellers. In winter in particular, groups of neighbours would gather to play cards, make music, or just to chat. It was customary to bring a sod of turf for the fire, and evenings would often conclude with dancing.

Ballydavid Studios are surrounded by working farms.

Many Gaeltacht musicians learnt their local styles of instrumental playing and singing by listening at such gatherings as children and in the same way folktales have been handed on from one generation to the next for millennia.

The custom of *bothántaíocht* was once common throughout rural Ireland, where pubs might start as 'rambling houses' before going on to get a licence to sell alcohol. Initially, these pubs were just family homes where neighbours would gather. In Corca Dhuibhne you will often see pubs with the word 'Tigh' as part of the name over the door. 'Tigh' means 'house' and these names literally translate as 'so-and-so's house', which is how local people still view them. They're not just businesses, they're also community gathering places and extensions of the owners' homes, an ethos that also defines Gaeltacht-based broadcasting.

THE GAA

An Cumann Lúthchleas Gael (The Gaelic Athletic Association, or GAA) is an Irish and international amateur sporting and cultural organisation which promotes traditional Irish sports, dance and the Irish language. Founded in 1884, it was associated from the outset with the country's cultural renaissance and its movement for political independence. Like many Irish cultural and political organisations at the turn of the twentieth century, it split and re-formed in accordance with the degree of separatism promoted by various factions within it. By 1888 it had consolidated and reached out to the Irish diaspora in the United States, where it still has a strong presence. Now, in the twenty-first century, it has more than 500,000 members worldwide. In Ireland its structure is organised on provincial and county lines, encouraging fierce, friendly rivalry on the playing field and providing a focus for community social interaction.

During the Irish War of Independence (1919–1921), when Irish cultural and sporting activities were severely curtailed by Britain, the GAA became a rallying point for nationalist resistance. As a result, the organisation became doctrinaire in its refusal to allow its membership to engage in 'foreign games': in 1938, after the setting up of the Irish state, it even removed Douglas Hyde, President of Ireland, from his position as one of its patrons for having, in his official capacity, attended a soccer match between

Gallarus playing field, home of the local GAA football team, An Gaeltacht.

Ireland and Poland. The rule Hyde had broken was rescinded in 1971, since when the Association has continued a process of building links with other sporting disciplines. In Corca Dhuibhne today, close to Baile na nGall, a rugby pitch that featured in the official 2015 World Cup video as the most westerly in Europe stands within 3km of the local Gaeltacht GAA team's home pitch, and young local players often belong to both clubs and practise both disciplines.

The GAA has a network of about 2,300 clubs throughout Ireland in which players who go on to represent their respective counties are trained and fostered through junior and senior levels by volunteers from their communities; young men and women also compete in their own local competitions up to finals at national level which are played in Dublin's Croke Park.

Specific counties are often associated with one or other of two GAA sports – football and hurling. Kerry is a football county; it's hard to spend time here without seeing kids and adults, male and female, wearing the distinctive GAA football jerseys – green and gold for the county or red and white for An Gaeltacht. The plaited colours can be seen dangling from cars' and vans' rear-view mirrors too; and on match days flags and painted messages wishing luck to various teams and individuals are often set up in schoolyards and along the roadsides.

Children outside Ballyferriter school, with the GAA's prestigious Sam Maguire cup, celebrate a County Kerry All-Ireland football victory.
COURTESY SUSAN UÍ BHEAGLAOICH

Sign at the rugby field on the Slea Head Drive beyond An Muiríoch.

11 Around Feohanagh

Feothanagh reed beds.
INSET: Wild foxgloves in June.

ALTHOUGH Baile na nGall translates literally as 'the town of the foreigners', the English form of its name on maps and signs is Ballydavid. This fact, confusing in itself, can become more confusing for visitors who follow the Slea Head Drive onwards and find another village with the English name of Ballydavid, situated beyond An Fheothanach (The Windy Place) near Ballydavid Head. The explanation, which is straightforward enough once you know it, exemplifies the potential effect of a colonial presence on local place names the world over. The village beyond An Feothanach is called

Dúinín Pier at low tide.

Baile Dháith in Irish, and its name translates literally as 'David's Town'. During the period of the Napoleonic Wars there was an English military outpost there which was subsequently transferred a few miles south along the coast, to Baile na nGall. From the authorities' point of view, the name related to the garrison, not the specific location of the village close to which it had been posted, so

An Mhuiríoch Dancehall poster from the 1960s.

the transfer of the military was accompanied by the transfer of the name. The fact that the relocation brought the English presence to a village which, in Irish, was already called 'the town of the foreigners' appears to be coincidental.

In the mid-twentieth century the hall in the village of An Mhuiríoch ('the seaside marsh') was a very popular dancehall, though, like the patterns that used to be held at holy wells and other locations, dances run by local

Baile Dháith, the original Ballydavid.

people were frowned on by the Church as likely to promote immorality. Ultimately some dances were taken over and run by the clergy but by the 1980s, with the growth of emigration and the ability to travel further for entertainment, dancing fell out of fashion.

Beyond the village of An Mhuiríoch the road leads north to Feothanach where the hall is the base for Aisteoirí Bhréanainn (Brandon Actors), a local drama group that has been presenting plays and entertainments in Irish since the early 1970s. For four decades the group has been assisted and encouraged by Fr Tomás Hickey, a former parish priest, who directed many of its productions and led it to success in national competitions and festivals.

The halls here now host a variety of such cultural and social events, from concerts and arts and crafts shows to coffee mornings and fundraisers. Their function is equivalent to that of a performing arts or social centre in city communities and, along with the pubs, they provide the area with spaces which are perfectly adapted to provide a continuous link to *bothántaíocht*.

CONVERSATION:
Vincent Gorman

In 2000, Vincent and Síle (Sheelagh) Gorman opened a purpose-built guesthouse and restaurant in a clifftop location below Mount Brandon called Glaise Beag (The Little Stream). The business grew naturally from the small café they had opened in their home in the 1980s, and from Vincent's family tradition of accommodating Irish-language students. Síle, who came to the area in the 1970s as an Irish-language student, works full-time as the hostess at Gormans' Clifftop House. Vincent, now an award-winning chef, is in charge of the restaurant.

❝ My family has been here on the same land way back beyond my great-grandfather's generation. When I was young it was a small farm with four cows and one pony. We used to make our own butter and that. We had hens and pigs and we'd grow potatoes and turnips. The pony would be used working on the farm and when the County Council were building roads my father would go drawing stone and that from the beaches for them, and he'd get extra for the pony. It would be unheard of back then for a man to be a cook. But when Síle and I were first working here in the kitchen together, there were too many knives hanging about, I suppose, so one of us had to go! When we opened up first it was out of necessity, nothing else but necessity. The 1980s were desperate here. There was no work. Nearly all my friends would have emigrated to America at that time and some of them never came back.

When I was younger my mother used to keep visitors who'd be round learning Irish, and she would have been feeding them. So I suppose I began by learning from that. It was all simple, fresh food. Things we'd grow and, back then, boats would come in here to the pier at Dúinín [Little Fort] when the men would be fishing for salmon and they used to have plaice and fish that they'd be

Dúinín Pier with Smerwick Harbour and The Three Sisters in the distance.

throwing away. They'd fire them up onto the pier and they'd be hopping there, and we used to go down and gather them up like windfall apples. We'd go home then and just gut them and put them on the pan. You couldn't get fresher.

In the early days we had no electric light or running water – I'd say that came in round the early 1960s. Every house then would have a barrel or two of mackerel and that would be the winter diet – potatoes and salted mackerel. In the summer you'd have carrots and parsnips, but in the winter the only vegetable besides potato would be turnip. I remember back then, in very, very bad weather, if there was a big swell in the harbour, there was so much fish round in those days that they'd get washed up on the beach. My father would go down with big bags and he'd bring them back full of fish, and what wasn't eaten would be salted. Pollock and wrasse and flat fish, they'd all be salted up and put in the barrel as well as the mackerel. You'd pick a lot of dillisk – edible seaweed – in those days, and periwinkles. We'd pick shellfish off the rocks and bring them home and cook them on the fire. That's how my mother cooked and she'd have been catering for twelve and maybe fourteen visitors sometimes.

When I was young we'd have bacon and pork but not everyone in the village would kill their animals at the same time.

Oystercatchers on the beach at Feohanagh.

So when one family would kill they'd share the meat around, and the next family would do the same thing and everyone would get some. We'd have no fruit back here then, no apple trees, say, but there'd be blackberries. And we'd have our own eggs and milk, and men out in the fields and that would drink a lot of buttermilk.

The landscape and the seascape round us dictate the food that I'd be working with today. In the past men would watch from the cliffs here, and when they'd see the salmon jumping they'd go out in boats and they'd make a ring around the salmon and they used to get over a hundred fish in one haul. No one's landing on the pier below any more but we'd still get our fish from local fishermen. We go out of our way to use local produce and we grow salads and vegetables here behind the house.

Kids in my day would play football but I suppose, when you think about it, it was a kind of rugby. We'd play on the roads and on commonage, and you'd have a couple of coats thrown down to mark the goals. But there were no rules and no training or teaching, we were just wild. You'd have the fist all the time when you were playing. And we'd have races up and down the cliffs – first down and first to the top. My God, if you'd see kids doing it now you'd call 999. We wouldn't be hunting for gulls eggs round here at all, it was just for recreation. We used to have games between schools and parishes then but that was crazy stuff – how anyone didn't get killed I don't know. We had no football field at that time. But then the GAA clubs got set up and

Schoolchildren in An Gaeltacht strip celebrate a
football victory. COURTESY SUSAN UÍ BHEAGLAOICH

Gallarus GAA pitch.

the Gallarus pitch was made. The club came first and then the
pitch. We had no hurleys – we couldn't afford them. I suppose
we made them sometimes out of bits of sticks. North Kerry
would be the hurling place. Football is the big thing here. The
girls are playing now too. They won the last two under-16 All-
Irelands for Kerry, which looks good for the future.

The rivalry between the Gaeltacht team and Dingle is huge.
You'd have to beat the townies. You need bragging rights locally
– that's the thing that really matters. But then, after that, you'd
be rooting for Kerry and you'd have players from the Gaeltacht
and Dingle town playing together. And you'd have local heroes. I
won the West Kerry under-14 medal with Páidí Ó Sé on the team.
The only medal I ever won. Even then you'd have known Páidí
was special. We all knew. He had the talent and he had all the
determination to make it.

Football training starts at national school these days. It starts
there – the teachers do great work. And now if you're involved in
clubs you'd have physios and doctors. And you'd have volunteers
out training the kids and getting on social media and tweeting
from matches. It's great, I think. There's a lot of young people
now involved in the Gaeltacht club. They're developing another
pitch – out collecting for it and planning to build it. You can't
wait, you have to go out and do it yourself. What happens here
is that the word goes out "we need tractors tomorrow" in Gallarus
or somewhere, and the tractors turn out. That teaches the kids

Winter clouds on Mount Brandon.

too, everyone sees that you have to put your shoulder to the wheel if you want to get things done. And if everyone feels they own it, they feel that they have to take care of it.

When I was young Mount Brandon wasn't marked – there were no paths then, it was a place for the sheep farmers. And there was so much work around houses you had no time to go walking. If you were going to school you still had your jobs at home. The henhouse had to be cleaned out and the calf shed had to be cleaned out. It was full on. The only day you had off, really, was the Sunday. And you had no way to go to matches then either. You might think of stealing the father's bike if he had one but you wouldn't get away with it. There was always something to do every day of the week. When my father wasn't out fishing he'd be out at two o'clock in the morning bringing up the catch from the pier before bringing it in to Dingle. The slip down to the pier then was too steep for the pony, so he'd carry up the bags on his own back. He might make two trips with the pony and cart into Dingle in a day and he'd get ten shillings or something for that – that was good money then. There was a lot of bartering went on at the time. My father grew good spuds and he'd barter them. But you needed the money too.

In the past sand was drawn from the beaches for building purposes.
COURTESY MÁIRE BEGLEY Ó SÉ

I remember when the television came we used to go to a neighbour's house and there'd be people all round outside, looking in through the window. And I remember the radios out on the windowsills and crowds gathered to listen to matches. There was a cinema over in Feothanach, beside the pub there. A clay floor and just benches. A fellow came around with the films – there was no electricity, he must have been working off batteries – and I saw the first film I ever saw there, *They Died With Their Boots On*. I saw it recently on television and I remembered every frame.

When I think of the things people used to use for entertainment – Bean an Droichead was a big thing for a while. The Woman of the Bridge. This local fellow used to go out in a shawl and he'd jump out when people would be walking the road. And the story went round. Who was it? Was it a ghost? The story spread like wildfire and everyone was asking who it was. That's what your man wanted. And then a couple of lads went out and waited for him. And caught him. It was the talk of the parishes. God, they had very little to do at that time! You didn't have the Internet so you made things up.

But ghost stories were a big thing. When there were no lights and you'd be walking the roads you'd believe them. Well, you'd be half-afraid and half-entertained by them. People talked to each other continuously those days and there was very little depression because there was no isolation. The villages were full of children. We'd wear no shoes during the week and the eldest girl in the village would have a bar of Lifebuoy soap and you'd go up to the river on a Saturday and she'd be there scrubbing all the kids' feet.

God, the speed at which things have changed is terrific. When I think of our own kids now, sometimes I need to pinch myself. The changes I've seen in, say, fifty years here are absolutely incredible. Everything still depends on work, though, and young people being able to find it. And, you know, like in my mother's time, it's still the case that the people coming here to learn Irish make a huge difference to the economy. But whatever you come for, there's so much here. You could stay around for a week and go out walking every day and you'd still be walking out to places that others don't go to. This place is still so, so wild and beautiful. 〃

The bridge at Feothanach.

Feothanach River and reedbeds with Mount Brandon reflected in the water.

The original foreigners who gave their names to Baile na nGall were probably Danes who – like the English who transferred the name Ballydavid from Baile Dháith – represented the settled presence of invaders. In the early Middle Ages Viking incursions were common all around the coastline of Ireland and, though the name Smerwick ('butter harbour') suggests trade rather than plundering, it is likely that the first Danes arrived armed and ready to fight. As it happens, the landscape they came to in this part of the peninsula offered the potential to produce weapons as well as safe harbours for their ships. The boggy flatlands here between the ocean and the mountain contain a rich source of iron.

Bog iron is a form of impure iron deposit that develops in bogs or swamps by the chemical or biochemical oxidation of iron carried in solution. In general, bog ores consist primarily of iron oxyhydroxides, commonly goethite. Iron smelting from bog iron was invented during the Pre-Roman Iron Age and practised extensively in the Viking era. In many parts of the world it remained important into the modern period, particularly to peasant iron production. In Russia, for example, it was the principal source of iron until the sixteenth century; and iron produced from bog ore was used for cannon balls by the colonial forces during the American Revolution.

But the principal exploitation of bogs throughout Irish history has been as a source of household fuel. Throughout the country, particularly in rural areas where trees were scarce, hand-cut peat (turf) had traditionally been used as fuel for generations, with

Turf-cutting demonstration at a Dingle Peninsula agricultural display.

families being allotted specific stretches of bog under the rundale system. In 1946 the government of the recently formed Republic set up a semi-state company to manage Ireland's peatlands. Its aims were to provide economic benefit for local communities and to achieve a home-grown energy supply by burning turf to produce electricity. This involved mechanised harvesting which took place primarily in the Midlands.

Peat forms when plant material, usually in wet areas, is inhibited from decaying fully by acidic and anaerobic conditions. It is composed mainly of wetland vegetation: principally bog plants, including mosses, sedges and shrubs. Most modern peat bogs formed in high latitudes after the retreat of the glaciers at the end of the last ice age some 12,000 years ago. As it accumulates, peat holds water, thereby creating wetter conditions, and allowing the area of wetland to expand. But it accumulates slowly, usually at the rate of about a millimetre per year, and both irresponsible harvesting on an industrial scale and bad management, such as overgrazing, can result in ecological damage.

Across the bogs under its control, the policies of Ireland's semi-state company, now called Bord na Móna, have produced both gains and losses of biodiversity. In 2010 and 2016 it released action plans to mitigate damage already done, and to plan for a future in which it will cease harvesting peat for electricity production by 2030. This move, involving the rehabilitation of tens of thousands of acres of bogland into new biodiverse habitats, is intended to enable the

Turf drying on a bog.

support of new ecotourism and community amenity resources. As part of the plan the company intends to locate sustainable businesses and activities on its bogs to promote renewable energy. These will include wind and solar projects, domestic fuel, biomass development, resource recovery and horticulture. From the outset, the plan – amounting to the biggest change in land use in modern Irish history – provoked fears that hand- and machine-cutting by individual farmers would be banned along with industrial harvesting.

Under the Wildlife (Amendment) Act, 2000, seventy-five areas of peatland of a type known as raised bogs were designated as Natural Heritage Areas, with the aim of protecting wildlife habitats, and a further fifty-three raised bog Special Areas of Conservation were designated under an EU Habitats Directive, which meant that turf could not be cut on them. Raised bogs are discrete, raised, dome-shaped masses of peat occupying former lakes or shallow depressions in the landscape. In Ireland they occur principally throughout the midlands.

In Corca Dhuibhne a type of peatland known as Atlantic blanket bog predominates and this type was not included in the designated areas, but the idea that traditional turf-cutting might be threatened elsewhere in the country produced expressions of solidarity. Heated demonstrations and negotiations took place over several years between turf-cutters' representatives and the Minister for Arts, Heritage and the Gaeltacht of the time, Jimmy Deenihan. In July 2016, after a period of review, it was announced that threatened habitats could more effectively be conserved through focused protection and a reconfigured network countrywide: this would deliver a long-term resolution for turf-cutters, while ensuring that Ireland meets its obligations under the Habitats Directive. Turf-cutters nationwide welcomed new legislation to de-designate thirty-nine raised bog Natural Heritage Areas and partially de-designate seven others, but stressed the need for ongoing consultation.

Within living memory in Corca Dhuibhne, every family spent time each year cutting turf, setting it in small stacks to dry in the wind, and then bringing it home from the bog in baskets strapped on donkeys. Once home, it was built up into large stacks to last as fuel through the winter. These might be kept under cover in sheds or built against house walls or back doors to provide insulation against wind and weather. Some villages in Corca Dhuibhne gained access to electricity as late as the 1970s so food was cooked on open hearths where several different turf fires could be kept going at once. This allowed the cook to regulate levels of heat under pans and kettles and a closed pot, known as a Bastable, in which bread was baked on the fire.

Turf burns with a particularly fragrant scent and, once lit, will continue to smoulder even when denied oxygen. Traditionally, the hearth fire would have been kept alight all year long, with the exception of the eve of Bealtaine, the cross-quarter day marking the midway point between the spring equinox and the summer solstice. On that night hearth fires were extinguished and subsequently relit from flames brought home from communal bonfires, a ritual intended to ensure the household's health and prosperity during the coming year.

The word Bealtaine, Irish for the month of May, is said to derive from 'Bel' and 'tine': Bel was the Celtic sun god, a promoter of fertility and healing, and *tine* in Irish means 'fire'. Dingle town's May festival, Féile na Bealtaine, is a modern echo of the Celtic calendar festival of

Beltane. Back west, many of the cross-quarter day's customs are still respected in individual households where farmers walk the circuit of their property and repair fences and boundary markers. On the eve of 1 May flowers are traditionally hung above doorways or scattered on doorsteps to bring blessings on inhabitants and livestock: traditionally, yellow blooms are chosen, suggestive of sunshine and light. In the past the communal fires became the centre of Bealtaine celebrations and ritual. Cattle were driven between two bonfires as a rite of purification and young men would leap the flames to bring good luck and fertility in the coming year. When hearth fires were rekindled from sods of turf brought home from Bealtaine bonfires, blessings were invoked on the household and the food that was to be cooked there.

Gorse, locally known as 'furze', and primroses on a ditch with Mount Brandon in the distance.

FLORA

In 1995 Oidhreacht Chorca Dhuibhne published *Flóra Chorca Dhuibhne: Aspects of the Flora of Corca Dhuibhne*, a splendid bilingual book, the product of four years' work by botanist Máirín Uí Chonchubhair and photographer Aodán Ó Conchúir, both natives of the area. Seldom seen in bookshops, it can still be purchased online and contains a wealth of information both for the interested visitor and the serious botanist.

Mount Brandon in February. The mountainous landscape here is largely treeless.

Many visitors to the peninsula are surprised by the lack of natural tree cover. This is explained by the fact that humans arrived here very early in the postglacial period. The first inhabitants, Mesolithic hunter-gatherers, arrived about 9,000 years ago and their presence did little to alter the landscape. But the Neolithic people who followed them about 3,000 years later were farmers who began a process of alteration, beginning with tree-felling, which has continued to the present day. There is a popular belief that Ireland's woodland was felled for timber to build ships for the British navy but in fact between 60 and 80 per cent of the native deciduous oak woods and pine forests had already been cleared before colonial interventions.

It is true, however, that shipbuilding intensified during the sixteenth century and the invention of the blast furnace led to iron-ore smelting that required large volumes of charcoal, which was produced by the controlled burning of coppiced wood. The mid-sixteenth century also saw the beginning of the Plantations of Ireland (c. 1556 – c.1690), when the English monarchy parcelled out large areas of land to English, Welsh and Scottish settlers who cleared forests to create pasture for livestock and tillage for crops. A subsequent fourfold increase in the population between 1700 and 1840 required further clearance to meet the increasing demand for food and shelter. Modern forestry is supported by the state and tends to consist of commercial coniferous planting.

For visitors today, two of the most noticeable wildflowers in the area are the scarlet and purple fuchsia and the neon-orange montbretia that grow profusely along miles of roadside here in summer. Though now emblematic of the Dingle Peninsula, both are relative newcomers. Fuchsia, a hybrid of garden origin, was first introduced here in about 1930. It rarely spreads from seed in Ireland but is widely planted as a durable and impenetrable hedge and will readily root from cuttings. Also a hybrid, montbretia, with its long, narrow leaves and tubular flowers, was introduced from South Africa at the beginning of the nineteenth century and is now naturalised all along the Atlantic seaboard. It spreads mainly by means of its corms but is also fertile. The vibrant colours of these two incomers are matched by the

A profusion of montbretia on a back road above Ballyferriter.

ABOVE LEFT: Fuchsia growing at An Riasc.

ABOVE: Montbretia, purple loose-strife and meadowsweet in a ditch at Gallarus.

LEFT: Yellow gorse flower.

ubiquitous gorse (locally called furze), a thorny evergreen shrub with golden flowers and a rich, coconutty scent, which has a longer history in the area as hedging.

A wealth of smaller, less evident wildflowers can be found on cliff and mountain walks. From Baile na Gall to Glaise Beag a 3km clifftop walk, listed by Condé Nast as one of the most beautiful in the world, offers stunning views of Ballydavid Head and Mount Brandon in one direction and across Smerwick Harbour to The Three Sisters on your return.

It is important to heed local advice with regard to the weather when you go walking, and to wear suitable footwear and clothing. Remember that there's a temperature drop of 2 to 3 degrees centigrade for every 300m you climb, so even if you set out in warm weather it will be significantly colder on a mountaintop. And if you do go climbing or take walks in isolated areas it's sensible to let someone know your planned route and estimated time of return. In case of emergency on a mountain call 999/112, ask for Mountain Rescue and be ready to give the clearest possible description of your location.

12 Brandon Creek

Mount Brandon has been a place of pilgrimage since before the coming of Christianity.

AS THE SLEA HEAD DRIVE begins to curve back towards Dingle town the dominant feature in the landscape is the huge mass of Cnoc Breannáin, Mount Brandon. It takes its present name from St Brendan the Navigator, whose Christian name in Irish is Bréanainn. The second highest mountain in Ireland (953m), it has been a centre of pilgrimage from time immemorial. Various derivations are given for the saint's name, one of which asserts that it comes from the Irish *Broen-finn* which means 'fair drop'. In Corca Dhuibhne today Bréanainn, as opposed to the anglicised Brendan or the Irish Breandán, is still a common given name for boys.

Prior to the assimilation of the area's pagan religious rites into the Christian tradition of pilgrimage, Mount Brandon was sacred to the Daghda, the 'Good God' and 'Lord of Great Knowledge' of the ancient Celts. One of the earliest pre-Christian Celtic deities, the Daghda, identified in some stories as one of the Tuatha Dé Dannan, is said to have control over life and death, the weather and crops, as well as time and the seasons. Sliabh Daghda (The Daghda's Mountain), which is Mount Brandon's pre-Christian name, is still sometimes used locally.

At the Slea Head Drive's most northerly point is The Churl's Creek, Cuas an Bhodaigh, known in English as Brandon Creek. The root of the Irish word for 'churl' here appears to be the Old Irish word for 'penis': as time went on the word *bodach* was used to denote 'an unmannerly giant' (where largeness was seen both as threatening and powerful), or simply 'a peasant' associated with the earth, as opposed to 'a gentleman'. The concept of the god who walks the earth disguised as a tattered, stupid or ribald old man is a common motif in global folklore and mythology and appears to be what is referred to here.

Stained-glass depiction of St Brendan in Ballyferriter Church by Kevin Kelly, dated 1999.

Moonrise over Brandon Peak.

The first mention of St Brendan occurs in the Irish chronicler Adamnan's *Vita Sancti Columbae*, written between AD 679 and 704: he is mentioned as a seafarer in the ninth-century *Martyrology of Tallaght*. He is said to have been born in Tralee in AD 484 and educated in a school founded by his foster-mother, St Ita. According to legend, Ita taught her pupils that the three things God most detested were 'a scowling face, obstinacy in wrongdoing, and too great a confidence in the power of money'.

Traditionally, Brandon Creek is the place from which, in AD 535, St Brendan and a group of companions set out on a legendary voyage in search of the Land of Promise of the Saints. The story of their adventures, called *Navigatio Sancti Brendani Abbatis* ('The Voyage of Saint Brendan the Abbot'), would subsequently become one of the best-selling books in medieval Europe.

The earliest extant version of the *Navigatio* was recorded around AD 900, though others probably circulated earlier. The book belongs to a genre of Irish stories, known as Immrama, which chronicle the journeys of saints and pilgrims in search of an otherworld situated to the west of Ireland and identified with the Christian paradise. Immrama echo an earlier pagan genre, known as Echtrae, in which heroes travel into the west in search of a land of eternal youth. In the Christian stories the travellers visit several islands on their journey and the wonders and inhabitants encountered there represent pagan challenges to their faith.

In the Christian Church, St Brendan is still revered as the patron saint of mariners. At the US Naval Academy in Annapolis, Maryland, he is depicted in a stained-glass window; the parish church in Ballyferriter also shows him in stained glass, holding a boat with a Celtic cross on its sail.

At Cuas an Bhodaigh today, set between two stones above the narrow creek which opens to a huge view of the ocean, a statue by Cliodhna Cussen of a bronze figure in a boat evokes the saint's

Cliodhna Cussen's sculpture of St Brendan The Voyager at Cuas an Bhodaigh.

departure on his voyage into the unknown. The concept of the immram itself evokes another emergence, from the confines of human perception into the boundless potential of the spirit.

St Brendan is said to have climbed Mount Brandon and prayed there alone before descending to prepare for his voyage. A nineteenth-century translation of the *Navigatio* describes how 'he proceeded to the remotest part of his own country … and there fitted up a tent, near a narrow creek, where a boat could enter. Then St Brendan and his companions, using iron implements, prepared a light vessel, with wicker sides and ribs, such as is usually made in that country, and covered it with cow hide, tanned in oakbark, tarring the joints thereof, and put on board provisions for forty days, with butter enough to dress hides for covering the boat and all utensils needed for the use of the crew.'

Over a hundred manuscripts of the *Navagatio* survive across Europe and in US libraries, and there were many medieval vernacular translations. One of the earliest is the twelfth-century Dutch *De Reis van Sinte Brandaen,* which may be derived from a lost High German text; numerous others include the early fourteenth-century Venetian version, *La navigazione di San Brandano,* and those in Alençon, France, and Barcelona, Spain. Some of the western end of the peninsula's monastic settlements may have been established or developed specifically to care for pilgrims travelling to venerate St Brendan or to continue a land pilgrimage by sea from the creek that was believed to have been the departure point of his voyage.

The *Navigatio* describes many vicissitudes and adventures experienced by Brendan and his companions and says that, having found the land they were seeking, they returned home to Ireland. There has long been a theory, based on rationalisation of the book's descriptions of their route, that the journey actually happened and that the land mass reached was North America. In 1976, convinced that the legend was founded in historical truth, the British explorer Tim Severin built a two-masted boat of Irish ash and oak, hand-lashed together with nearly two miles (3km) of leather thong, wrapped with forty-nine traditionally tanned oxhides and sealed with wool grease. In it, he and a crew of four sailed 4,500 miles (7,200km), from Brandon Creek to Peckford Island, Newfoundland, stopping at the Hebrides and Iceland en route. *The Brendan Voyage,*

Severin's account of the expedition, became an international best-seller, has been translated into sixteen languages, and is the subject of a major orchestral work by the Irish composer Shaun Davey.

In 2013 Domhnall Mac Síthigh, a poet, carpenter and voyager who was born and raised in Ballyferriter, published *Iomramh Bhréanainn MMXI (The Brendan Voyage 2011),* a book about his experiences on a sea voyage to Iceland following the path of St Brendan. In 2016, along with a crew of four others, he completed the last stage of a sea pilgrimage to Santiago di Compostela in Galicia in north-western Spain, the destination of one of the most popular European pilgrimages of the Middle Ages. The voyage, made in a *naomhóg* built by Mac Síthigh and Liam Holden, another member of the crew, is chronicled in a three-part television series for TG4 by Anú Pictures in association with Phoenix Films for broadcast in spring 2017. The series is called *Camino na Sáile*, which means 'Camino by Sea'.

Liam Holden is a painter whose art is primarily influenced by the sea. The other crew members were Breanndán Ó Beaglaoich (Brendan Begley), a traditional musician who was born and lives back west and whose family's musical inheritance reaches back generations, and Breanndán Ó Mhuircheartaigh (Brendan Moriarty), a stonemason and folklorist, also from the area. Because Ó Mhuircheartaigh was unable to make it for the entire 2016 leg of the Camino, the Dublin-born Oscar-winning singer-songwriter Glen Hansard joined the crew as his substitute. Camino na Sáile was completed in three summer voyages, with each leg of the pilgrimage starting from where the previous one had ended. It finished with the crew of the *naomhóg* carrying their craft to the steps of the Cathedral of Santiago de Compostela.

Domhnall Mac Síthigh

Domhnall Mac Síthigh believes that his fascination for voyaging is inherited from his mother's ancestors, who were seafarers. For him, love of the sea is inextricably connected with love of the western end of the peninsula where he and his wife live and have raised their family in a house built on land farmed by his father's people for generations.

❝ According to legend, St Brendan and his companions were joined on their voyage at the last minute by a *bodach* – a churl – who demanded to be allowed to accompany them. He was a trickster, a joker, a storyteller. He wanted to go with them and Brendan took him on board because such a man was wanted on the voyage. And he would be. You'd need someone of the kind. That's the story but the character is very ancient. No doubt the *bodach* was there long before St Brendan.

It's hard to know why something like Camino na Sáile happens. You're going into great danger and I don't think you're ever able to tell yourself why. You never have the answer. But it comes from a love of the sea. Love of your own place – the hills and the cliffs and the mountains and the sea. When you're at sea there's always a connection with the place you came from. Your mind is always going back to it.

When I was young the first job I had was picking periwinkles. You'd pick them and sell them. Half a crown a stone. And at the time the fishermen would be coming home in *naomhóga*. I was there one day and two boats were going out after dinner and they took me into one of them. I suppose they took pity on me because of the way I was looking at them. I was there in the front of the *naomhóg* and I was frightened. The waves were going over

The relationship between the ocean and the landscape are an enduring part of the Gaeltacht's spiritual heritage.

my head nearly, and the gunwale was nearly under water, and I was terrified altogether. But I was so happy. It was two men from the [Great Blasket] island took me out. I've never forgotten it.

'Then, as for my voyaging, I made many a voyage before the Camino. Around Ireland. Across the Atlantic in a Connemara Hooker. To Spain that way as well – from Dublin to Santander. And other voyages. One from Trieste down to the Adriatic and the Mediterranean and back to Connemara. And one from Dingle in 2011, up to Shetland and on to the Faroe Islands and across to Iceland and back again to Dingle. I suppose there was spirituality involved in all of them.

Mount Brandon is very important to me. Before I take such a voyage I'll constantly go up Mount Brandon by way of preparation. Before going to Iceland I'd say I went up and down Mount Brandon at least twenty times. It made me think. It made me remember. It prepared my mind. Because it's so hard. You have to focus your mind and your soul – everything. And you have to strengthen your body.

If you're awake three nights and three days at sea dealing with bad weather you have to be fit. Not just physically but mentally. You have to be quick thinking. When you walk alone to prepare yourself you think of how your ancestors took those same paths up the mountain. You think about God. I do that. I believe in God. I suppose many people don't, but I do. I believe that there's another life in which the people who died before us live, and that they're still all around us. And I believe that if I trust them they help me.

The first voyages I made, they weren't pilgrimages, as such, but explorations. I'd always have holy water with me in a boat. Often I'd have a little stone I'd have picked up on the mountain. And I'd pray to St Brendan to bring us through safely. Before my first long voyage I'd read the *Navigatio* many times and I couldn't understand what St Brendan meant when he said that he left it to God to direct their course on the sea. I couldn't get my head around that in any way. But I gained an understanding of it when I was out there voyaging myself.

It was when we were coming back from Heimaey Island, which is off Iceland, and making for St Kilda which was 500 miles away, and that would take five days and nights. We were about 100 miles from St Kilda, doing well till a gale of wind came up. The captain, Paddy Barry, said we hadn't enough power to fight it. We'd have to let the boat go with the wind. So we tied down everything on deck and went down into the cabin and secured the hatches, and there were five of us below there and what Paddy said to us then was "nothing lasts forever". And we were all

Mist on Mount Brandon. In Irish folklore, mist is associated with magic and transformation.

stretched on our bunks and not a word out of any of us. We were being thrown about on the sea by the wind and I was saying to myself, "this is the end now. We won't come safe out of this." I had a diary with me, with my name and my address in it. And I said to myself that maybe it would be washed up on some shore and someone would find it and it would be sent home, and they'd know what had happened to me. I was certain it was the end. The sea was so fierce. We had no idea where it might take us. And then I thought of St Brendan and how he left it to God to bring him safely through. When I remembered that, my fear left me. And I fell asleep. You don't sleep if you're frightened. But I did, I'd say I slept for an hour. The wind blew for twelve hours without letting up, but it didn't bother me. Everything was thrown about. I think I read a page or so of a book when I woke, but you couldn't read really. So I slept again. And then, when the wind finally dropped, we went up on deck and we'd been driven 40 miles in the opposite direction, away from St Kilda. That was the time that I realised that I'd never be afraid again and I understood what St Brendan meant when he said that he'd left it to God. That frees you.

A view of the ocean from above Brandon Creek where the explorer Tim Severin launched his attempt to prove the practicality of St Brendan's legendary voyage.

There's a difference between fighting against the odds and winning as a voyager and winning a game or a competition if you're an athlete. When you're the victor at sea you've beaten no one. No one's left crying. You've done something remarkable, but what you've been fighting is the sea itself and the weather and fear – and even ignorance. You learn something. About yourself and about the world you live in.

As for the Camino, that's different again. There's a tradition of pilgrimage there and it goes back thousands of years. There's the *naomhóg*, she's called the *Naomh Gobnait*. There's the fact that Liam and I made it ourselves. In Irish you don't say that you built a *naomhóg*. You "build" a boat because you build it from the keel up, like you build a house from the foundations. But you "make" a naomhóg because you start at the top and work down. Well, we had that boat. We'd done other long voyages in her. The first was in 2012. She's wonderful under sail. That's the thing about a *naomhóg*. It has no keel and if the wind blows from the right direction you can sail her so easily and comfortably at sea. You could almost take a nap when you're at it. It was the monks, I suppose, who developed that craft and there's hardly been any change made to its design since. We tried to make a change once, to improve the steering. And it didn't work for us. We reverted to the traditional design.

People are very important. Before I leave this place it's important that people bless me and wish me well. There are people who say they'll pray for me. That they'll light a candle for me. I know one man who will keep a candle lit here without ever quenching it throughout the whole voyage. Such things help you and give you energy. The energy crosses the space between you. Another important thing – I think I learnt this from going up Mount Brandon – is that you must never complain. You can't complain on a sea voyage. It doesn't matter what pain you might be in or how much other people might be upsetting you, or whatever happens, you mustn't complain. You must take pleasure in everything or you lose the energy that sustains you.

You're so close to the water. You feel every wave and that's wonderful. But it's so taxing, from the point of view of rowing, and it can be so dangerous that often we'd ask ourselves where we get the energy. We're not young. But, then again, I don't think I'd have been able to do it thirty or forty years ago. It's a particular kind of energy. I think myself it has a lot to do with the fact that the nights we'd spend on land during the Camino were spent in tents, not houses. You're inside in the tent and you hear the rain and you feel the wind outside and you're aware of it. You hear the seagulls in the morning and you see the dawn. If you were inside in a comfortable room you wouldn't see or hear those things. When you're in a tent you can still hear the sea – you hardly leave it. And you're in touch with the earth like the *naomhóg*'s in touch with the sea.

Then, when I come home, I find I don't want to meet or talk to anyone. That's when it's very important to go up Mount Brandon again. To leave the sea behind me and walk on the earth again. I suppose it brings you to a different way of thinking. It turns you around and brings you to a different state of mind. Something like that – I don't know really. These things are complicated and that's the point. They make you think and they affect you. There's a saying in Irish that there are three things that are magical – music, fog and sailing. I'd say myself that sailing in a *naomhóg* is the most magical of the three.

A magical summer sunset over the Atlantic seen from Clogher Head.

NAOMHÓGA

A *naomhóg* is an Irish boat with a wooden frame over which greased animal skins were stretched as a covering. These days the covering is of tarred canvas or calico. The vessels are light enough to be carried upside down on the crew's shoulders. Traditionally used along the Atlantic coastline, they are also called currachs and sometimes canoes: the name *naomhóg* (plural: *naomhóga*) is used in counties Kerry, Cork and Waterford.

The design of the *naomhóg* has varied across time, from place to place and according to usage, but uniformly the boats are sturdy, light and versatile vessels. The framework consists of latticework formed of rib frames and longitudinal slats, surmounted by a gunwale. There are stem and stern posts, but no keel. Thwarts are fitted with knees (braces). Cleats or thole pins are fitted for the oars, and there may be a mast and sail, though with a minimum of rigging. The seats are stationary and the oars are non-feathering – that is, they don't widen out at the tips – so the boat can cut through the choppy waters of the Atlantic.

Lightweight boats of this kind, called coracles, were in use all over Ireland throughout history and prehistory, but the sea-going *naomhóg* was not common in Corca Dhuibhne until the late

A racing *naomhóg* at the Fionn Trá regatta, 2013.

The annual Fionn Trá regatta was revived by the local community in 1994.

A women's team compete in a racing naomhóg.

Naomhóg at Ventry Pier.

Blasket islanders loading a cow into a naomhóg.

nineteenth century. Before then, the vessel used both by mainland fishermen and the Blasket islanders was the heavy wooden seine boat, which required eight men to row it and required a backup boat, called a '*foilár*', possibly from the English word 'follower'. The seine boat's name derives from the 'seines' or dragnets used when fishing from it. Used for carrying loads and livestock as well as for fishing, the working *naomhóg* appealed particularly to the island boatmen because it could be handled by a crew of three and was less cumbersome to beach than the seine boat.

These days fibreglass craft similar in shape to the traditional vessels are often seen, sometimes powered by an outboard motor. Timber and canvas *naomhóga* continue to be made by craftsmen like Domhnall Mac Síthigh and Liam Holden, however, and highly popular annual regattas all round the peninsula ensure that new crews of oarsmen and women continue to learn the ancient skills of handling them.

Mount Brandon from Feothanagh.

A project to seek out and map the traditional place names on Mount Brandon has been initiated by Oidhreacht Chorca Dhuibhne and is ongoing. Pilgrimages to the summit of the mountain are traditionally made on 16 May, the feast of St Brendan, and on the last Sunday in July, known locally as 'Crom Dubh's Sunday' or *Domhnach Chruim Dhuibh*. Crom Dubh, or Crom Cruach, is thought to have been the earliest solar/agricultural god worshipped in Ireland, possibly predating the ancient Celtic sun god Bel who also appears in the mythology of the British Isles as Lugh.

The meaning of Crom Dubh's name is hard to establish; Crom means 'crooked' or 'stooped' and 'Dubh' means 'black', suggesting a sinister presence. But Crom can also mean 'a chief or leader'. 'Cruach', meanwhile, can be interpreted as relating both to blood and to a corn stack, suggesting violence – perhaps sacrifice – but also fertility and plenty. He is therefore linked to grain agriculture, which arrived in Ireland in the fourth or third millennium BC. In another form of Crom's name, 'Cenn Cruach', the word 'Cenn' means 'head', possibly referring to the ancient reverence for the head as the centre of knowledge. Some scholars link the character of Crom with the

Daghda, the ultimate controller of life and death in Irish mythology, through his control of the weather and the seasons.

In Corca Dhuibhne, tradition has it that St Brendan asked Crom Cruach, a rich pagan chieftain, for money to build a church. Instead, Crom sent the saint a wild bull, hoping it would kill him. But Brendan tamed the bull by prayer and, astonished, Crom asked him for Christian baptism. Before baptising him, Brendan punished Crom by burying him for three days, leaving only his head above the ground. This legend appears to be a Christian echo of a struggle between the god Crom Dubh and the later pagan deity Lugh, also worshipped as a solar/agricultural god. Lugh's name is the root of the Irish language word for both August and the fourth season of the ancient Celtic calendar, which is Lughnasa. The seasonal festival of Lughnasa is celebrated all over Ireland with festivities taking place from late July through August. Its traditional dancing, feasting, bonfires, horse races and music-making easily lend themselves to recreation as arts festivals and tourist attractions, and it's often marketed via its association with the Irish playwright Brian Friel's 1990 play, *Dancing at Lughnasa*, which was filmed in 1998 starring Meryl Streep.

Horse races on beaches at Lughnasa may relate to ancient horse-swimming rituals to honour the sun god.

The Brandon Range in winter. Like many societies globally, the Celtic spiritual tradition sees high places as the home of the gods.

In Corca Dhuibhne the festivities that take place on the summit of Mount Brandon on the last Sunday of July celebrate Lughnasa as the victory of Lugh, who strode up the Daghda's mountain when the corn was ripe to slay Crom Dubh with his spear of light. But the festive day is still referred to not as Lugh's but as Crom Dubh's Sunday, suggesting that both St Brendan's humiliated pagan chieftain and Lugh's dark, crooked enemy are memories of an ancient Lord of the Harvest who may have required blood sacrifice and was invoked to avert famine. Just as the Daghda's name is preserved in the local name for Mount Brandon, Crom's is preserved locally in the assertion '*dar Chruim*' – literally 'by Crom' – which is often used in conversation to mean 'by God'.

13 The way back to Dingle

Western flank of Mount Brandon.

WHEN YOU LEAVE CUAS AN BHODAIGH, the Slea Head Drive takes you through some of the western end of the peninsula's wildest and least inhabited countryside and back towards Dingle town. Though there is a welcoming pub to stop at, you won't find restaurants or coffee shops between this point and the town itself. Having traversed the loop that has taken you out to Slea Head and around through Ballyferriter, Feothanach and Cuas an Bhodaigh, the route back into Dingle hugs the western flank of the Brandon range. The back roads off it are relatively deserted and wonderful for walking and cycling.

Legends such as St Brendan's, and older stories like that of the *bodach* who may not be what he seems, belong to a time when the arrival of an unexpected traveller was a source of new stories which, folded into the local storytellers' repertoire, became part of Corca Dhuibhne's rich oral heritage. The return of an emigrant or of an itinerant labourer – known in Ireland as a *spailpín* – had the same effect. This balance between what can be called native to an area and what has been assimilated by it is a delicate one, instinctively addressed by oral cultures throughout the world by careful attribution of provenance to stories, songs and music. In the Irish tradition, tunes and songs are usually introduced or concluded by the words 'I got that from so-and-so, or from such-and-such a book or recording', and the breaks in music sessions are often spent discussing different versions of tunes and remembering what singers or players from the past were associated with them.

Looking across Smerwick Harbour from above Cuas an Bhodaigh with a glimpse of the Blasket Island group.

Mary Ellen Begley (née Lynch) from Baile na bPuc (Goats' Town) died in Dingle Hospital on 20 July 2004 at the age of eighty-eight. Her parents, Kate Ferris and Pat Lynch, were musical and her grand-uncle, Tom Ferris, was a celebrated traditional fiddler. A prevailing family memory is of Mary Ellen tapping out complex rhythms on the kitchen table with her fingers or the bread knife as she prepared meals for a household of up to fourteen members, which included three generations. She was famous for her dancing at parties in the family farmhouse, attended by everyone from neighbours to visiting Irish-language academics, students, musicians, itinerant farm labourers and Travellers walking the countryside offering to mend pots and pans. She is also remembered for her ability to calm cattle and her spirited use of both Irish and English in battles of verbal wit. Both Mary Ellen and her husband, Brendan Begley, who owned the dancehall in Muiríoch, were singers, and their musical talent was inherited by their nine children who, in turn, have passed it on to a new generation.

Breanndán Ó Beaglaoich (Brendan Begley), one of the crew of the *Naomh Gobait* on the sea pilgrimage to Santiago di Compostela, is Mary Ellen's youngest son and a virtuoso on the accordion. Like his siblings – among them the international recording artist Séamus – he learned to play and sing at home and cut his teeth as a stage performer in his father's dancehall. As a child, he was taught to step-dance by his mother, and to waltz in the yard outside their home to the sound of a neighbour playing music from the far side of the river.

After a period as a teacher in Dublin, Breanndán became a professional musician, making solo albums as well as recording with groups including The Boys of the Lough, Beginish, The Chieftains, Stockton's Wing and Seán Davey. He toured the US, where he played in Carnegie Hall, hosted by Garrison Keillor. Along with his sons Bréanainn, Cormac and Conchubhair and his daughter Cliodhna, he played in Cape Breton in Nova Scotia in October 2009, at the Celtic Cuban Festival in April 2010, in Moscow in 2010, and in venues all over Ireland. He has also performed extensively with the traditional Irish fiddler Caoimhín Ó Raghallaigh. And, in 2016, Ó Raghallaigh performed in Ireland's National Concert Hall and toured nationwide with Brendan's son, Cormac, a concertina player.

The experience of Mary Ellen Begley's children exemplifies how traditional Irish music has blossomed since the 1950s, turning what was once seen as an unsophisticated and almost obsolete form into an international phenomenon. Breanndán and his sisters and brothers were among the young musicians featured in the early years of Raidió na Gaeltachta and what is now TG4, as well as on RTÉ, and this hitherto unavailable exposure of traditional material and performers from Gaeltacht regions did much to stimulate wider national interest. Since then, increased ability to share music files globally from personal devices has contributed to global awareness of the form, stimulated by the success of groups such as The Chieftains and of stage shows such as *Riverdance*, which originated as an interval performance act during RTÉ's hosting of the 1994 Eurovision Song Contest.

In 1960 the Irish composer Seán Ó Riada set up Ceoltóirí Cualann (The Cualann Musicians), a traditional group which included many of the founding members of The Chieftains. Ó Riada, who held positions on the staff of both RTÉ and Ireland's national Abbey Theatre, was a regular visitor to Corca Dhuibhne, where he studied the Irish language and *sean-nós* singing with Seán de hÓra of Cloichear. '*Sean-nós*', which literally means 'the old style' or 'the old way', is used to describe a form of singing and dancing which, by the 1960s, was flourishing almost exclusively in Irish-speaking communities. As well as offering a new domestic platform for traditional music, Ó Riada, who was classically trained, was among the first recording artists to commit these traditional tunes to paper, and to orchestrate them.

Established in 1962, The Chieftains featured a sound that was largely based around the traditional Irish uilleann pipes and strongly influenced by Ó Riada's orchestrations. By 1975 the ensemble included Derek Bell, a classically trained performer on several instruments and a former professor of harp at the Academy of

'Uilleann' means 'elbow': air is pumped into the pipes by the player's elbow.

Seán Ó Riada's work was seminal in reviving traditional Irish music.

Music in Belfast. Part of Ó Riada's intention in setting up Ceoltóirí Chualann had been to revitalise the work of the blind harpist and composer Turlough Carolan (1670–1738) who – apparently uniquely for his period – had also married traditional Irish music with classical influence. Carolan's music, then less recognised, is once again a familiar part of the traditional Irish repertoire. In 2011 Caitríona Rowsome published *The Complete Carolan Songs & Airs* (Waltons Publishing), a collection of 226 airs that gives a unique perspective to Carolan's music and songs, combining his surviving airs with harp settings and metrically matching them with his own lyrics, along with English-language interpretations. Caitríona, an Irish harpist and the descendant of four generations of uilleann pipers, was born in Dublin and now lives in the village where her mother was raised.

By the 1980s a sense of what constituted 'Irish' music had shifted towards the traditional repertoire and away from groups like the Clancy Brothers, whose songs and ballads had been popularised by the American folk-music revival that began in the 1940s with the work of performers such as Pete Seeger and Woody Guthrie, and peaked in the 1960s with that of Bob Dylan and Joan Baez. But to suggest that the Gaeltacht musical tradition is more authentically Irish than that of performers like the Clancy brothers is oversimplification. Many of the tunes and the majority of the jigs, hornpipes and other dance music heard in the Gaeltacht have their origins in English and Scottish material introduced by British soldiers and itinerant dancing masters in the eighteenth and nineteenth centuries; and polkas – also presumably introduced by the soldiery and central to the Corca Dhuibhne repertoire – originated in nineteenth-century Bohemia, now part of the Czech Republic. Nevertheless, traditional, as opposed to folk or country, Irish music has deep roots in a specifically native sensibility. Unaccompanied *sean-nós* singing, in particular, represents an age-old inheritance that has been handed on in a purely oral tradition for centuries.

Páidí Mhárthain Mac Gearailt

**Páidí Mhárthain Mac Gearailt
has lived all his life within a few
miles of the village of Márthain
on Cruach Mhárthain, the home
of his father's people. One of
Ireland's most admired *sean-nós*
singers, he regularly visits
schools in Dingle, handing on
his cultural inheritance of song.**

❛ In the past around here the music and the songs were seen as
separate. You wouldn't listen to tunes being played at all. Music
was for dancing and songs were for listening to. That's changed
completely. I suppose there's far less dancing and now people are
all for sitting down listening to musicians. I remember back then
too that there were pubs for songs and others for stories and
talking. There'd be a lot of singing in Begley's pub in Ballydavid
when I was fourteen or fifteen. As lads we'd be up and down the
pier there, and you'd be in and out of a canoe maybe, a big gang
of us. And I used go over to Begley's, to the window – I wouldn't
be allowed inside – and I'd be listening. The other lads wouldn't
know what I was at, but I was drawn
to it. Maybe it'd be a fellow with a
voice like a crow but I'd be fierce
interested. There's a bit of magic in it.

In Irish you'd never say 'sing a
song', you'd say "*abair amhrán*" and
that means "say a song". That's what
you do, because you're telling a story.
And, you know, sometimes I find that
the story changes in my head when
I'm saying the song. Like, there's one
particular song and the girl and the

A November sunset at the
pier by Begley's pub in
Ballydavid.

boy are going away. And sometimes she goes with him and sometimes in my head she doesn't. Before I start saying that song I always say to myself, "I wonder what's going to happen?" Because I never know until the last verse. And a few verses before the end I'm saying in my head, "I wonder will she go with him at all?" Sometimes I ask myself why I can't just make up my mind before I get up and say the song. I could tell myself, "this time, now, she's going to go with him." But no, I find I can't do it.

But then, there's an old saying "*tá dhá insint ar gach scéal*"– "there's two ways of telling every story". And that saying ends "*is tá dhá rá dhéag ar gach amhrán*" – "and there's twelve ways of saying every song". You have to go through it from beginning to end to know which story you're telling today. That's why you have to sing the whole of it. I was singing up in Dublin in a pub one time and the barman came up to me and he said, "there's no singing here." Well, I had my eyes closed because I was singing but I could see him all the time. And I said to myself, "I'll finish my story anyway and he can throw me out after – well, he can try!" And he stood before me and he said, "I told you, there's no singing here." I kept the eyes closed but I was there ready, in case he'd come at me. But I finished my song and there were other singers there, a few from Connemara, and they appreciated what I'd done. You wouldn't blame him. He was only a barman and he had some rule. But they knew what I was doing. I wanted to finish my song so that the story would be finished and I'd have it told.

I don't know that I like competitions. I suppose that it's good that they're there but there's ifs and buts about it. Anyway, one time I was up singing in a competition and the judge interrupted me and she said, "you can stop now." She'd heard enough, she said. To her it was just a competition. There was no story involved. And that's not right. And you'd get that thing now in competitions where they'd be going in for them and they'd be feeling they'd have to perfect a song. It'd have to be perfect. But there's no such thing as perfection. You're learning all the time. And you can't learn anything if you're afraid of getting it wrong.

When I'm teaching kids in the schools now I want them to make their own of the song. OK, you have to learn it, but I always

Fishermen at work at Dingle Pier.

say, "when you have it learned now, you can make your own of it." I tell them they should be able to say "that's the way I tell that song." I think it's so important. Because, first of all it makes it more interesting for yourself, and then if it comes out from you naturally it's beautiful. "Live the song", that's what I say to them.

I hated school myself. I left when I was fourteen, I just didn't like it. But back when I was ten or eleven, one of the teachers was sick for a long time and there was no such thing as substitute teachers then. So the master would send one of us in to keep an eye on the younger ones. And I'd be there with the little kids of six or seven and I'd always have them singing. Kids will get bored with anything eventually, that's natural but, for the forty minutes or the hour or so, there they'd be, singing away for me, and they'd be happy out. And the master would be delighted because he'd hear them singing and he'd know they weren't blaggarding inside in the room or behaving badly. But I never did my Inter Cert. I just wrote my name on the paper and walked out of the exam.

I remember then I went working down the pier loading fish, and there was a lot of fish and we were doing well and I got £18 that day, which was a pile of money at the time. And I was saying to myself, "Isn't this better than going to school when I'd have no pound in my pocket?" And there was a while then when I was out fishing myself, and I went driving a fish lorry, but mostly now I'd be buying and selling fish, working for different people locally.

My father and mother would always be singing around the house when I was young. My father would be invited to a lot of ball nights when they'd want a good singer to break the ice before everyone would do their party piece. And my mother was always singing when she'd be cooking or sweeping the floor, or whatever she was doing. She'd be singing – not humming now or anything, but singing. And back then there'd always be kids running in and out of each other's houses. I remember all the elderly people round here loved kids – and what I was thinking about that was maybe they'd lost their own kids through emigration. There were people emigrating from here aged fifteen and sixteen then, so they made pets of the small children while they had them. I have grandchildren myself now in Australia and I don't know what we'd do without the phones and FaceChat. But they come back and forth now as well, and you couldn't do that in the past. They make nothing of distances these days.

My own grandmother was a great storyteller. Her father came from Cahersiveen, down around Valentia Island, and they'd have different songs down there. He'd come in fishing into Ballydavid and the fishermen would bring different songs – or the same songs but different ways of singing them. I'd have a few songs myself from there, and I'd have heard some of the old people from that area singing. They'd have beautiful Irish in Cahersiveen and back in those days they'd always be back and forth fishing.

I remember being told that when you'd have people from here going down as spailpíns to Tipperary and Cork they'd always be waiting for them to come back, because they'd have a new song. "So and so is away now and he'll be home after the harvest, and I guarantee you he'll have a good song now when he's back again." That's the way a good few songs came in. And we had people that went to the States and they'd send songs back and they'd bring songs back, and everyone would learn them. My own head would be full of songs all the time. I'd be saying them in my head when I'd be driving or anything. I might have a hundred songs, or I suppose I might have more than that, and they come back to me when I say them, even if I don't remember I have them. I'd have a picture in my mind of Cruach Mhárthain if I'd be up on a stage or wherever, saying a song, because that was where my father

Cruach Mhárthain, the mountain from which Páidí Mhárthain takes his name.

was from. That's what I see in my head, and my mind would be inside in the song.

One of my own heroes would be Séamus Ó Muircheartaigh who was from Ard na Caithne. He went away to America and he never came back. But he wrote songs and he sent them home and when I was young, I don't know how it was, but everybody had them. And I read about him and it said that he'd sent money to Pádraig Pearse before 1916, when Pearse had an Irish-language school up in Dublin. Over $100 he'd collected and he sent it to him. So I wanted to know more about his songs because I'd read that, and I'd heard my father talking about him. He never came home but he sent his wife back – she was a Hussey from Riasc – and his two sons came with her. I went out a while back myself to Butte, Montana – I was asked to go out and sing there with Méabh, Séamus Begley's daughter – and Ó Muircheartaigh had been there and he'd written about that place. I found that very moving. Songs that had been written over there and had come back home to Ireland, and I was bringing them back again. That would be the kind of thing that would drive me on.

I don't think you can force anything on anyone, whether it's the music or the Irish language or anything. And I didn't think I was really interested in going into the schools teaching at first, because I hadn't liked school myself. But they asked me, and when I went in I loved it. I love kids anyway. And, I suppose, if you have something you want to pass it on, you want to share it. And, as a kid, if you enjoy something you'll make it your own, you see, and I like that.

THE TRADITIONAL MUSIC SESSION

Traditional pub music sessions are organic gatherings: they're relaxed, friendly and convivial and you never know what combination of instruments will arrive on any occasion. People ramble in, order drinks at the bar and wander over to join the musicians, who gather around the fire or at a table. There might be fiddles, accordions, concertinas or whistles. Sometime there will be pipes or a flute. People often bring several instruments and swap from one to another for different tunes. Sometimes there is a bodhrán, the traditional Irish skin drum which may have developed from vessels used for winnowing: some scholars, including Seán Ó Riada, identify it as native to Corca Dhuibhne and believe it to have a musical history which predates Christianity.

Conventionally, Irish traditional music is played in unison, not harmonised, and one result is that, to an outside eye, new arrivals appear just to pick up the tune and join in whenever they feel like it. But like everything else in Corca Dhuibhne, pub music-making involves courtesy and etiquette, which is mostly understated. Decisions are made with no more than a nod or a glance, but the sequence of tunes is always led by the senior member in the group, who also calls for people to sing or to play solo. New tunes

A pub session in Tigh Uí Mhurchú, Ballyferriter.

THE WAY BACK TO DINGLE

and their sources are valued. People will want to know where you learnt a particular variation, where it came from and who taught it to you. Joining a pub session is a wonderful experience. You will be welcomed and, if the musicians are local, you'll be drawn into a dynamic living tradition that stretches back across centuries.

But you might want to sip your drink at the bar for a while before you sit down with your bodhrán or tin whistle. And if you haven't joined that group before, it is correct to wait to be asked before you start playing. Many pubs are still seen as extensions of the owners' houses so, basically, what you need to remember is that you are a guest in somebody's home.

Pub music-making tends to be interrupted now and then by breaks for conversation but, generally speaking, sessions consist of far more playing and singing than talking. If Irish is being spoken by the group when you arrive, people may switch to English out of courtesy. Indicating that the switch isn't necessary will always be appreciated, even if it happens anyway; and if the conversation becomes bilingual you may find yourself in the perfect circumstances to begin to pick up a little Irish or to improve your fluency.

While positive in many ways, the ease with which tunes can now be shared electronically can erode the specificity of local styles in music-making. In 2004 Scoil Cheoil an Earraigh (The Spring Music School) was set up in Baile an Fheirtéaraigh by Breanndán Ó Beaglaoich and Niamh Ní Bhaoill, a television producer who lives locally, and whose company Sibéal Teo has originated many music programmes for TG4. Their aim was to celebrate and to hand on the traditional music style of Corca Dhuibhne. The five-day school continues to hold about twenty-five classes in a wide range of instruments annually, and also runs workshops in *sean-nós* singing and dance. There are also concerts, sessions, singers' nights, recitals, a pupils' concert, a guided walk and other events based on various aspects of the area's tradition and, while every effort is made to ensure that no one feels marginalised, Irish is the language of all the school's classes and events.

Breanndán Ó Beaglaoich, playing during Scoil Cheoil an Earraigh in 2012.

Students and teachers relaxing outside the museum in Ballyferriter during Scoil Cheoil an Earraigh in 2012.

Central to the tradition of *sean-nós* is the custom of passing on tunes by ear and not on paper. Yet, by chance, alongside the oral tradition, much of the western end of the peninsula's musical inheritance is preserved in an outstanding manuscript collection of some 2,300 mainly traditional tunes painstakingly gathered in the area by James Goodman (1828–1896). Goodman, a canon of the Church of Ireland, was born in Ceann Trá, where his father was a rector and, in 1879, became Professor of Irish in Trinity College Dublin. An Irish speaker from childhood, and an accomplished singer and uilleann piper, Goodman became an avid collector of the tunes he heard from local musicians, most of whom were probably born in pre-Famine Ireland. In some cases he made transcriptions from live performances, particularly in the case of Tom Kennedy, a local uilleann piper who became a personal friend; he also drew from manuscripts and other printed sources that have since been lost.

In a significant collaboration between the Library of Trinity College Dublin and the Irish Traditional Music Archive (ITMA), Goodman's six manuscript volumes of tunes and song texts have recently been digitised and made freely available to a worldwide audience through a dedicated website (goodman.itma.ie). Four of these volumes were presented to the university's library on Goodman's death, and a further two (including the words for some of the tunes) in 2006, after they were rediscovered by one of his descendants.

Traditional singer and instrumentalist Muireann Nic Amhlaoibh with her daughters in her home near Ballyferriter.

While children learn music and *sean-nós* songs from their school-teachers, and from practitioners like Páidí Mhárthain, the tradition of listening and learning in the home continues in many families, and singing and music-making is still a central part of family and communal gatherings.

The Slea Head Drive takes you back to Dingle town through a remarkably varied landscape. The rugged mountains of the Brandon range are to your left, on your right is a mix of forestry, rich pastureland and, beyond it, the bulk of Sliabh an Iolair and Cruach Mhárthain guarding the end of the peninsula. Ahead of you are Dingle Harbour and Dingle Bay. Just before the roundabout at Milltown Bridge is the modern building where Údarás na Gaeltachta has its offices.

* * *

There's a story told on the Dingle Peninsula, which is said to predate the Spanish Armada and to contain within it a song that may, or may not, be older still. Once, when a woman was gathering seaweed on a beach below Ard na Caithne, a foreign ship came into the bay and a sailor took the woman. Her brother was a fisherman, and he spent weeks and months searching for her though all the ports of the world. But he never found her.

Ard na Caithne and The Middle Peak.

Then, one day, as he passed a house in the Basque country in Spain, he heard a woman's voice there in the house singing. The rhythm of her song was the rhythm of the waves at sea. And it named the places where the fiercest waves would break around Ard na Caithne.

'May God keep your father from The Raven and his Mother, from the Little Peak and the Middle Peak', she sang, as she rocked a cradle. 'From the Goat Fold of the drowned waves', she sang, as he stood and listened. 'And from Binn Diarmada of the ugly teeth', she sang as he broke the door down.

Her brother went up the stairs then. And he went up into the high room where the woman sat singing to her baby. And he took them away out of that house, and brought them back home to their village.

> *Go seachnaí Dia t'athair ar an bhFiach is ar a Mháthair*
> *Ar an mBinn Bhig is an an mBinn Mhéanaigh*
> *Ar Chúl na nGabhar na dtonnta báite*
> *Is ar Bhinn Dhiarmada na fiacaile ghráinne.*

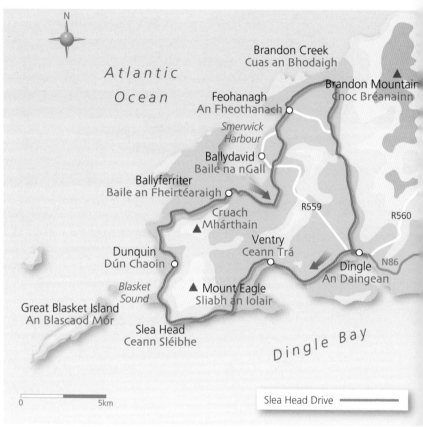

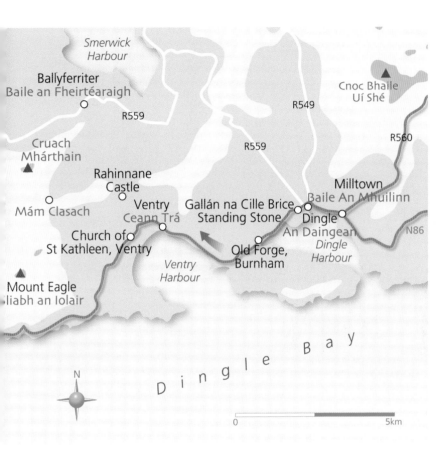

Smerwick
Harbour

Ballyferriter
Baile an Fheirtéaraigh

R559

Cnoc Bhaile
Uí Shé

R549

R560

Cruach
Mhárthain

R559

Rahinnane
Castle

Milltown
Baile An Mhuilinn

Mám Clasach

Ventry
Ceann Trá

Gallán na Cille Brice
Standing Stone

Dingle
An Daingean

N86

Church of
St Kathleen, Ventry

Old Forge,
Burnham

Dingle
Harbour

Ventry
Harbour

Mount Eagle
Sliabh an Iolair

D i n g l e   B a y

N

0   5km

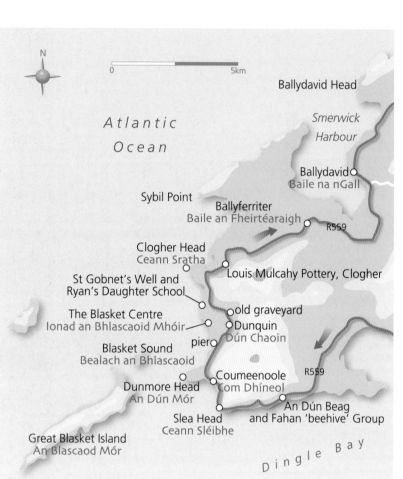

N

0   5km

Atlantic

Ocean

Brandon Creek
Cuas an Bhodaigh

(Old) Ballydavid
Baile Dháith

Feohanagh
An Fheothanach

Dooneen Pier
Cé an Dúinín

An Ghlaise Bheag

The Three Sisters
An Triúr Deirféar

Smerwick
Ard na Caithne

Ballydavid
Baile na nGall

Murreagh An Mhuiríoch

Sybil Point
Ceann Sibéal

Dún an Óir

Smerwick
Harbour

Béal Bán Beach

GAA field

Kilmalkedar
Cill Mhaoil Chéadair

Golf Course

museum

Ballyferriter
Baile an Fheirtéaraigh

An Riasc

Gallarus Oratory

R549

Clogher Head
Ceann Sratha

Ballineanig
Baile an Éanaigh

R559

Cruach
Mhárthain

Ventry
Ceann Trá

Dingle
An Daingean

N86

Dunquin
Dún Chaoin

Blasket
Sound

Mount Eagle
Sliabh an Iolair

R559

Slea Head
Ceann Sléibhe

Dingle Bay

PRONUNCIATION GUIDE

(Note: The letters 'ch' are used in the indicated pronunciations here to represent a sound common in Irish but not in Standard English. It is pronounced as in the German name 'Bach' or in the Scottish pronunciation of 'loch'.)

1. DINGLE TOWN

Sliabh Mis	Shleev Mish
Cnoc Breannáin	K'nuck BRAYnaw-in
Sliabh an Iolair	Shleev un OLLir
Cruach Mhárthain	CROOach VARhin
Blas na hÉireann	Blos na HAIRann
Tá cúpla focal agam	Haw COOpla FUHkul aGUM
Go raibh maith agat	Guh roh mah aGUT
Slán	Slawn
Dia dhuit	DEEa gwit
Féile na Bealtaine	FAYleh na BeeOWLt'nne
Lugh	Loo
Lá an Dreóilín	Law un DROHleen
Pádraig Ó Fiannachta	PAWrig Oh FEEnoch-ta
An Café Liteartha	Un CAfay LITer-ha
Daingean Uí Chúis	DANGan Eee KOOish

2. MILLTOWN AND BURNHAM

An Gorta Mór	Un GURta More
Coláiste Íde	CullAWSHteh EEdeh
Clochán	CluhHAWN
Gallán na Cille Brice	GallAWN na KILleh BRIkeh

3. VENTRY

Corca Dhuibhne	KURka GWEEna
Com Dhíneoil	Kowm yeeNYOE-il
Cosán na Naomh	cussAWN na Nave
Gaeltacht	GWALEtukt
Gaeilgeoirí	GwaleGORee
Ainmhithe Ag Trasnú	ANNveh-heh egg TRASSnoo
Bean an tigh	Ban un TEE
Ceann Trá	KeeOWNE Traw
Fionn Trá	F'yoon Traw
Cumann na mBan	KUMan na Mon
Séamas Ó Luing	SHAYmus Oh Ling
Cath Finntrágha	Kah F'yoonTRAW

Fionn Mac Cumhaill	F'yoon M'Kool
Dara Donn	DARRa Down
Glas Mac Dreamhain	Gloss Mok Drown
Conn Crithir	Kon KRIhir
Crea	Kray
Caol	Quail
Meitheal	MEHill
Údarás na Gaeltachta	OOder-awse na GWALEtoch-ta
Comharchumann Forbartha Chorca Dhuibhne	KOREkum-an FURbur-ha CHURka GWEEna
Coláistí Chorca Dhuibhne	KullAWEshtee CHURka GWEEna
Oidhreacht Chorca Dhuibhne	EYErocht CHURka GWEEna
Ard a' Bhóthair	Ord a VOhir
Caitlín	KathlEEN
An Clasach	On ClassACH
Mám Clasach	Mawm ClassACH
Dún Chaoin	Doon Queen

4. AROUND SLEA HEAD

An Dún Beag	On Doon Beg
An Baile Uachtarach	On BOLLyeh OOacht-ar-uch
Bollach	B'llACH
Naomhóg	NaveOGUE
Tomás Ó Cinnéide	TomAWSE Oh KinEHdeh
Ar Seachrán	Air ShochRAWN
Dún Mór	Doon More
Músaem Chorca Dhuibhne	MooSAY'm CHURka GWEEna

5. DUNQUIN

Scoil Naomh Gobnait	Sgol Nave GUBnit
Máire Ní Mhaoileoin	MOYreh Nee VwaylOWE-in
Breandán/Máire Feiritéar	BrownDAWN/MOYreh FairTARE
Micheál Ó Dubhshláine	MEEhaul Oh DooHLOYNuh
Cliodhna	KLEEoh-na
Domhnall Mac Síthigh	DOEnal Mok SHEEhig

6. THE BLASKET CENTRE

Pádraig Ó Siochfhradha	PAWdrig Oh SHUCKrah-da
An Seabhac	Un SHAOWoch
Ionad an Bhlascaoid Mhóir	UNud an VLAScade VOHir
Piaras Feirtéar	PEErass FairTARE

Inis Tuaisceart	INish TOOSHkyart
An Fear Marbh	On Far MARiv
Tomás Ó Criomhthain	TomAWSE Oh KRIhin
An tOileánach	On TillAWNoch
Brian Ó Ceallaigh	Bree'n Oh KYALig
Allagar na hInise	OLagar na HINish-ih
Máire Ní Chinnéide	MOYreh Nee KinEHdeh
Baile an Bhiocáire	BOLLyeh On VICoy-reh
Beag Inis	BegINish
Dáithí de Mordha	DAWhee deh MORga
Rí	Ree
Pádraig Ó Catháin	PAWdrig Oh KaHOYN
Fiche Blian ag Fás	FIheh Blee'n egg Fawse
Ní Bheidh Mo Leithéid Arís Ann	Nee veg muh lehHADE arEESH aown
Ní bheidh ár leithéidí arís ann	Nee veg awr lehHADEee arEESH aown
Tír na nÓg	Teer na NOGUE
Oisín i ndíaidh na Féinne	UshEEN ih nee'g na FAYneh

7. FROM CLOGHER TO THE THREE SISTERS

Cloichear	KLOhur
Ceann Sibeál	KeeOWNE ShihBALE
Dún an Óir	Doon on OHir
Dún an Áir	Doon on AWEir
Gort a Ghearradh	Gurt a YARRah
Gort na gCeann	Gurt na Gyowne
Maidhc Ó Mainín	Mike Oh ManEEN
Binn Diarmada	Been DEERma-da
Binn Méanach	Been M'YANach
Binn Hánraí	Been AownREE
Binn Shean-Draoi	Been HaownDREE
Dáithí Ó hÓgáin	DAWhee Oh HOgaw-in
Dinnseanchas	DinSHANNchas
An Buailtín	On BoolTEEN

8. BALLYFERRITER

Baile an Fheirtéaraigh	BAL'n AirTAREigh
Máire Mhac an tSaoi	MOYreh WOKatee
A Bhean Óg Ón ...	A Van Ogue OWN ...
Séamas Eoinín Feirtéir	SHAYmus OYNeen FairTARE

9. AROUND RIASC

Béal Bán	BEEal Bawn
Más é ár lá é, 'sé ár lá é	Maws eh are LAW eh, shay are LAW eh
Baile Eaglaise	BOLLyeh AGleh-sha
Gearóid Mac an tSíthigh	GarODE Mock un TEEhig
Lughnasa	LOOna-sa
Tomás Ó Suilleabháin	TomAWSE Oh SULEa-voyn
Baile an Éanaigh	BOLLyeh'nAYNEig
Duine eile imithe	DINih el' IMih-heh
Púcaí	PooKEE
An Riasc	On REEask
Cill Mhaoil Chéadair	Kill Vyaol KAYdir
Gall Ioros	GALLirras
Ciarraighe	KeerEE
Ráth Sheanáin	Raw HENoyne
Tuatha Dé Danann	TOOhah Day DANawn
Bóthar na Marbh	BOHhar na MAR'v
Sidhe	Shee
Aos Sí	Ace Shee

10. BALLYDAVID

Baile na nGall	BOLLyeh na n'ngowl
Ard na Caithne	Ord na CAHne
Raidió na Gaeltachta	RAHdi-o na GWAYLEtoch-tah
Sáirséal agus Dill	SARshale ag-ass Dill
Rinn Ó gCuanach	Rine Oh GOOan-ach
Scéal Foilsitheora	SHKEEal File-shaHOAREah
Dara Ó Cinnéide	DAra Oh KinEHdeh
An Saol Ó Dheas	On SAIL Oh Yass
Baile na hAbha	BOLLyeh Na HOWah
Cuas an Bhodaigh	KOOass on VODig
Teilifís na Gaeilge	Te-leFEESH na GWAYLEgeh
Bothántaíocht	BuhHAWNtee-ocht
Bothán	BuhHAWN
An Cumann Lúthchleas Gael	Un KUM'n LOOchlass Gwayle

11. AROUND FEOHANAGH

An Fheothanach	On YEOha-noch
An Mhuiríoch	On VuirEEoch
Aisteoirí Bhréanainn	AshTORee VRAYnaw-in
Glaise Beag	GLASHih Beg

Dúinín	DoonEEN
Bean an Droichead	Ban 'n DRIHhid
Bord na Móna	Board na MOANa
Bealtaine	BeeOWLt'nne
Máirín Uí Chonchubhair	MawREEN Ee CHUNuhCHOOir
Aodán Ó Conchúir	EhDAWN Oh CHUNuhCHOOir

12. BRANDON CREEK

Daghda	DIEdah
Sliabh Daghda	Shleeve DIEdah
Camino na Sáile	KamEEno na SAWleh
Domhnach Chruim Dhuibh	DOWnoch Chrim Gwiv
Crom Dubh	Krum Duv
Crom Cruach	Krum KROOach
Dar Chruim	Dar Chrim

13. THE WAY BACK TO DINGLE

Spailpín	ShpalPEEN
Baile na bPuc	BOLLyeh na Buck
Caoimhín Ó Raghallaigh	QueeVEEN Oh RAhal-ig
Seán Ó Riada	Shawn Oh REEahda
Ceoltóirí Cualann	KeowlTORee KOOal'n
Sean-nós	Shan NOE'SS
Uilleann	ILLann
Páidí Mhárthain Mac Gearailt	PAWdee VARhin M'GARalt
Abair amhrán	OB-ur OWrawn
Tá dhá insint ar gach scéal	Haw gaw EENshint air goch SHKEEal
Is tá dhá rá dhéag ar gach amhrán	Iss haw gaw raw YAYug air goch OWrawn
Méabh	Mave
Scoil Cheoil an Earraigh	Sgol KeeOLE on ARig
Niamh Ní Bhaoill	Neeve Nee Vweel

FURTHER READING

Maps and Guidebooks

Discovery Series: Kerry 70. Sraith Eolais Ciarraí. Ordnance Survey Ireland, 2015

The Dingle Peninsula: A Walking Guide. Adrian Hendroff. The Collins Press, 2015

The Dingle Peninsula. Steve MacDonogh. (New edition revised and updated by Camilla Dinkel and Mike Venner). Utter Press, 2013

Archaeology, Flora and Geology

Archaeological Survey of the Dingle Peninsula/Suirbhé Seandálaíochata Chorca Dhuibhne. Judith Cuppage. Oidhreacht Chorca Dhuibhne, 1986

Flóra Chorca Dhuibhne. Aspects of the Flora of Chorca Dhuibhne. Máirín Uí Chonchubhair and Aodán Ó Conchúir. Oidhreacht Chorca Dhuibhne, 1995

Kerry: A Natural History. Terry Carruthers. The Collins Press, 1998

Local History

Travels in Wicklow, West Kerry and Connemara. J. M. Synge. Illustrated by Jack Butler Yeats. Interlink Publishing Group, 2005

Green and Gold: The Wrenboys of Dingle. Steve MacDonogh. Brandon, 1983

Bibeanna: Memories from a Corner of Ireland. Brenda Ní Shúilleabháin. Mercier Press, 2007

www.duchas.ie/en The National Folklore Collection of Ireland is one of the largest folklore collections in the world. Material from 26 counties in its Schools' Collection is available via its website, where scans and transcriptions of material collected in schools can be accessed via a Search facility.

www.logainm.ie/en/ The place-names database of Ireland (established with The Placenames Branch, Department of Arts, Heritage, Regional, Rural and Gaeltacht Affairs). Interactive site providing information on local *dinnseanchas/logainmneacha.*

Logainmneacha Dhún Chaoin. Éamonn Ó hÓgáin agus John Kennedy. Comharchumann Dhún Chaoin, 2017.

The Brendan Voyage: Sailing to America in a Leather Boat to Prove the Legend of the Irish Sailor Saints. Tim Severin. Modern Library, 2000

The Voyage of St Brendan. John J. O'Meara. Dolmen Press, 1981. (A translation from the Latin of the *Navigatio Sancti Brendani Abbatis*)

https://thomaspatrickashe.files.wordpress.com/2014/09/noraashewitnesssta tement.pdf The statement made in 1952 to The Bureau of Military History by Nóra Ághas, sister of the hero of the 1916 Rising, Tomás Ashe (Ághas), who died on hunger strike in 1917.

The O'Rahilly: A Secret History of the Rebellion of 1916. Aodogan O'Rahilly. The Lilliput Press, 2016

Troubled Epic: On Location with Ryan's Daughter. Michael Tanner. The Collins Press, 2012

Fan Inti. Domhnall Mac Síthigh. Coiscéim 2014 (*Naomhóga, a stair agus a ndéantús* – Naomhogues, their history and construction)

Myths and Legend

Over Nine Waves: A Book of Irish Legends. Marie Heaney. Faber & Faber, 1995

Gods and Fighting Men: The Story of the Tuatha De Danaan and of the Fianna of Ireland. (Coole ed. Lady Gregory's Works, vol. 3) Lady Gregory. Colin Smythe Ltd, 1987

History

The Celtic Realms: The History and Culture of the Celtic Peoples from Pre-history to the Norman Invasion. Myles Dillon and Nora Chadwick. Phoenix Press, 2000

The Celts: A Chronological History. Dáithí Ó hÓgáin. The Collins Press, 2006

The Course of Irish History. T. W. Moody and F. X. Martin. Mercier Press, 1967

Pilgrimage in Ireland: The Monuments and the People. Peter Harbison. Syracuse University Press, 1995

Eleanor Countess of Desmond. Anne Chambers. Gill & Macmillan, 2011

The Downfall of the Spanish Armada in Ireland. Ken Douglas. Gill & Macmillan, 2010

The Famine in the Dingle Peninsula. Kieran Foley. (In *The Atlas of the Great Irish Famine*, eds. John Crowley, William J. Smyth and Mike Murphy.) Cork University Press, 2012

Irish Country Houses: A Chronicle of Change. David Hicks. The Collins Press, 2013

Cumann na mBan and the Irish Revolution. Cal McCarthy. The Collins Press, 2014

Music and Song

An Blas Muimhneach. Breandán 'ac Gearailt. Coiscéim, 2007 (songs and information about 'An Spailpín' Séamus Ó Muircheartaigh.)

Seán Ó Riada: His Life and Work. Tomás Ó Canainn. The Collins Press, 2003

The Complete Carolan Songs & Airs, Arranged for the Irish Harp. Caitríona Rowsome. Waltons, 2011

Ceol Duibhneach. Breanndán Ó Beaglaoich & Niamh Ní Bhaoill. Sibéal Teo, 2009

The Story of Irish Dance. Helen Brennan. Brandon, 1999

The Blasket Islands

The Western Island. Robin Flower. Oxford University Press, 1978

The Irish Tradition. Robin Flower. The Lilliput Press, 1994

Island Home: The Blasket Heritage. George Thomson. Brandon, 1998

The Blasket Island Guide. Ray Stagles and Sue Redican. The O'Brien Press, 2011

The Islandman. Tomás O'Crohan. Oxford University Press, 2000

Peig: the autobiography of Peig Sayers of the Great Blasket Island. Trans. Bryan MacMahon. Talbot Press, 1983

An Old Woman's Reflections: The Life of a Blasket Island Storyteller. Peig Sayers. Oxford University Press first published 1962, reissued 2000

Twenty Years A-Growing. Maurice O'Sullivan. With an introduction by E. M. Forster. Oxford University Press first published 1937, reissued 2000

From the Great Blasket to America: The Last Memoir by an Islander. Michael Carney and Gerald Hayes. The Collins Press, 2013

The Loneliest Boy in the World: The Last Child of the Great Blasket. Gearóid Cheaist Ó Catháin with Patricia Ahern, The Collins Press, 2014

The Last Blasket King: Pádraig Ó Catháin, An Rí. Gerald Hayes with Eliza Kane. The Collins Press, 2015

Inishvickillane. Micheál Ó Dubhshláine. Brandon, 2009

Méiní: the Blasket Nurse. Leslie Matson. Mercier Press, 1996

The Great Blasket/An Bhlascaod Mór: A Photographic Portrait/Portráid Pictiúr. Dáithí De Mórdha & Micheál De Mórdha with Ciarán Walsh, photo ed. The Collins Press, 2013.

An Island Community: The Ebb and Flow of the Great Blasket Island. Micheál de Mórdha. Trans, Gabriel Fitzmaurice. The Liberties Press, 2015

Memoir

Coitianta ar mo Pheann. Caitlín Ní Mhaoileoin, Bean Uí Shé. Coiscéim, 2011

The Wild Rover: The Autobiography of Tomás Ó Cinnéide. Trans. Pádraig Tyers. Mercier Press, 1997

House Don't Fall on Me. Maidhc Dainín Ó Sé .Trans Gabriel Fitzmaurice. Mercier Press, 2007

Dúthaigh Duibhneac. Breandán "Brandy" Mac Gearailt. *Griangrafanna* (photos) Mike Shaughnessy. Coiscéim, 2014. (Photographic collection with reminiscences from individuals back west.)

Acknowledgements

The authors would particularly like to express their gratitude to Dáithí de Mórdha, formerly of the OPW Blasket Centre, for his provision of archive photographs, and to Isabel Bennett, who allowed us to photograph the famine boiler in Músaem Chorca Dhuibhne. We are also grateful to Máire Begley Ó Sé for allowing us to photograph memorabilia from Halla na Muirí.

Our thanks are due to the staff at Dingle's Fáilte Ireland Office and Dingle Library and to The Dingle Peninsula Tourism Alliance, Comharchumann Forbortha Chorca Dhuibhne, Oidhreacht Chorca Dhuibhne and Údarás na Gaeltachta for much-appreciated help and information. We are also grateful to William O'Brien and Nick Hogan of University College Cork's Department of Archaeology, to designers Alison Burns of Studio 10 Design and Terry Foley of Anú Design; and, as ever, to our literary agent Gaia Banks at Sheil Land Associates Ltd.

Lobster pots.

INDEX